Hidden Sussex

A new anthology for Sussex

Fiction, non-fiction and poetry from the
Black, Asian and Minority Ethnic experience

A Writing Our Legacy publication

Editors: Umi Sinha, Dean Atta and Colin Grant

Writing Our Legacy, Community Base, 113 Queens Road, Brighton BN1 3XG http://writingourlegacy.org.uk

Printed by One Digital (Digaprint Ltd)
www.one-digital.com

Book cover design by Donna Ambarita
linkedin.com/in/donna-ambarita

ISBN 978-1-9161290-0-9 (paperback)
ISBN 978-1-9161290-1-6 (ebook)

Supported by Arts Council England

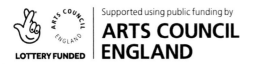

Supported using public funding by
**ARTS COUNCIL
ENGLAND**
LOTTERY FUNDED

Annie Richardson's 'Weaving the Threads' is adapted from her blog posts 'Picking at the Seams' and 'Still Weaving the Threads' https://earlyyearsannie.home.blog/

Jenny Arach's poems 'At Home with the Queen' and 'Brighton Beach' were first published in the *Ink on My Lips* anthology, Waterloo Press, 2013.

L Oluwafemi Hughes Jonas's 'Beyond Borders' references The Boomtown Rats song 'I Don't Like Mondays' and Nina Simone's songs 'Mississippi Goddam' and 'Ain't Got No/I Got Life'.

Nina Thaddeus's 'From Sindh to Sussex – My Mother's Memories' contains extracts from *I Love to See You Eat* by Nina Thaddeus, CreateSpace Independent Publishing Platform, 2017.

Alinah Azadeh's 'The Unmarked Box' references Rumi's poem 'Unmarked Boxes'. *The Unmarked Box*, 2010 and *Gifts of the Departed (II)*, 2009, by Alinah Azadeh appear courtesy of the artist.

Ingrid Pollard's *Seaside Series*, 1989 appears courtesy of the artist.

Jill Carpin, *Alternative Sussex Day Flag*, a new commission for Writing Our Legacy, 2019 https://www.jillcarpin.com/

Josef Cabey, *Hidden Sussex Map*, a new commission for Writing Our Legacy, 2019 www.josefcabeyart.com

Contents

Hidden Sussex Map

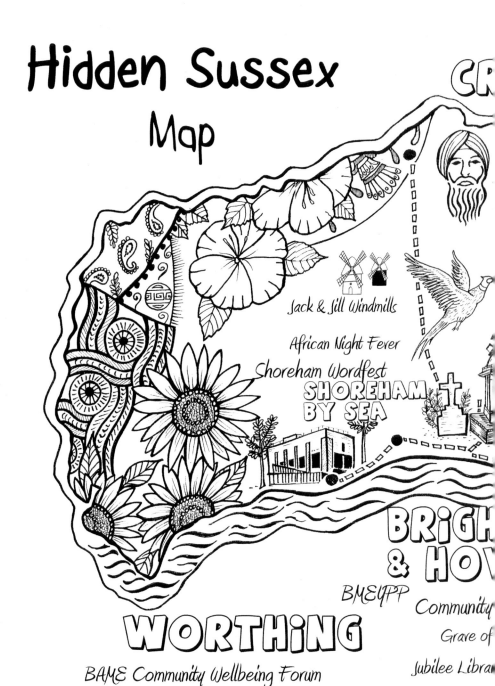

CR...

Jack & Jill Windmills

African Night Fever

Shoreham Wordfest

SHOREHAM BY SEA

BRIGH & HOV

BMEYPP

Community
Grave of
Jubilee Libra...

WORTHING

BAME Community Wellbeing Forum

New Writing South

S...

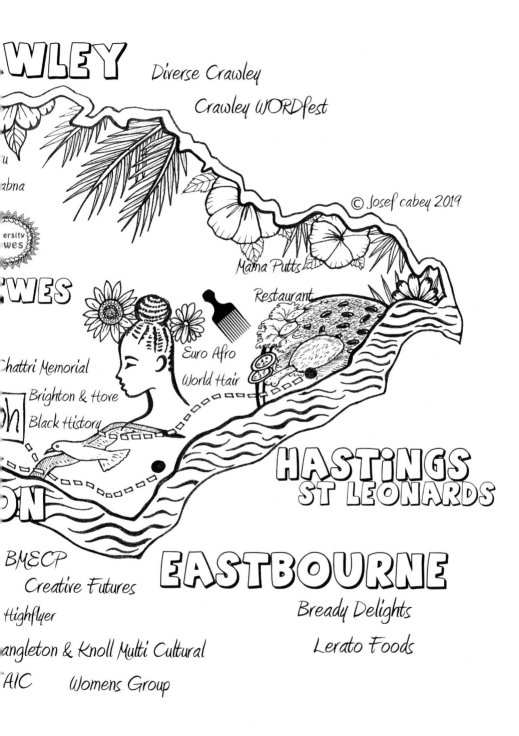

WLEY

Diverse Crawley

Crawley WORDfest

u

abna

© Josef cabey 2019

ersity
wes

WES

Chattri Memorial

Brighton & Hove
Black History

Euro Afro
World Hair

Mama Putts

Restaurant

h

HASTINGS
ST LEONARDS

ON

BMECP
Creative Futures

Highflyer

angleton & Knoll Multi Cultural

AIC   Womens Group

EASTBOURNE

Bready Delights

Lerato Foods

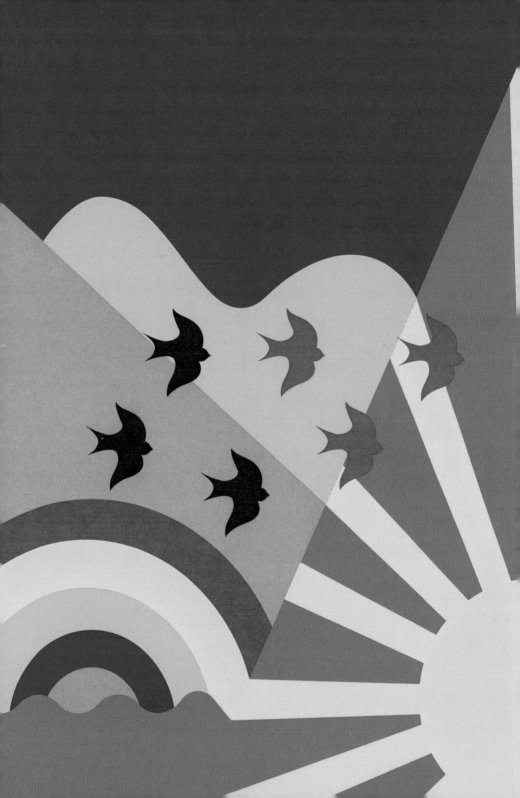

Introduction

The Hidden Sussex anthology reimagines the Sussex landscape from the Black, Asian and minority ethnic perspective – BAME, BME, or whatever labels describe our communities. One label does not fit all, and we hope that this book will help people to understand why.

Twenty-three writers have been selected for our anthology, featuring 27 works, through an open call in autumn 2018 followed by a series of workshops across the county.

Our contributors come from across East Sussex, West Sussex and Brighton, including Crawley, Uckfield, Eastbourne, Lewes, Hastings, Brighton and beyond.

The anthology tells stories of many firsts – of first trips to Afro-Caribbean hairdressers, first sexual awakenings, first visit to the Chattri Memorial. The writing also deals with middles and ends – raising children, solitary pursuits, deaths of friends and family.

We are transported to local places of interest such as Cuckmere Haven and Brighton Pavilion, and also elsewhere – to Pakistan, India, Iran. Some authors deal with pressing issues of contemporary Britain, including Brexit and the Windrush scandal, while others cast their eye over history and the natural environment.

There are three inspirations for this anthology.

'Creating a home and community'

Firstly, this book was born out of my personal experience.

I first moved to Brighton in 2000 and found myself looking for a community. I was newly settled in the UK (recent transplant from New York City), with no friends in town. I grew up as a mixed-race Mexican-American from a working class family who experienced racism and marginalisation in the US.

With Brighton, I couldn't have discovered a better place to be. I met inspiring writers, artists and community leaders who are friends today such as Umi Sinha, Sarah Naomi Lee, Bert Williams MBE, Sharon Otoo and others. I also learned about internationally renowned writers living locally, including John Agard, Grace Nicholls and many others.

Having opportunities to meet others and help contribute to Brighton's diverse community has made a huge impact on me.

Hidden Sussex is Writing Our Legacy's first publication. This is an important achievement for a grass-roots BME literature organisation that started in 2012 and operates with no paid staff.

I hope this sense of 'community' for artists, creatives and everyone of colour will continue to exist – helped by books like ours.

'But there are no Black people in Brighton'

Secondly, I wanted to create a vehicle for social change, to help shift perception about the Black experience in Sussex. Starting with, Brighton and Sussex is not all white. There are many people of colour here, who were born and grew up here, and many more are moving here from London and elsewhere.

When I moved to Brighton, people used to tell me 'oh there are no Black people in Brighton!'. It used to piss me off. But I realised there was a disconnect between the way that I – as a mixed-race person – saw and experienced the world and how others experienced it.

In 2000, the BAME population of Brighton was 10%. By 2010, the population had risen to 13-15%. Brilliant, I thought. While I was overjoyed with the statistic and the clear visibility of people of colour around Brighton, I knew most people in our community were still dealing with the same lack of diversity awareness, racism, discrimination, marginalisation and other issues that a so-called progressive liberal city like Brighton & Hove should not be experiencing. The same is true in 2019.

'Black people don't go camping'

In 2013, the late artist Irene Mensah said at one of our Black History Month group meetings, 'Someone told me 'Black people don't go camping'. I don't think that's true. I like camping, do you?'. We spent hours discussing the other 'Black people' stereotypes. Did you know, Black people don't eat pasta?

It's not news that BAME people are underrepresented in publishing and in most white-collar sectors in the UK such as academia, media, creative arts … the list goes on.

While it's been heartening to see recent campaigns to improve Black representation in publishing, such as independent publisher Jacaranda's #Twentyin2020 initiative, diversity-focused The Good Literary Agency, and many publishing opportunities to support diverse writers, it doesn't feel that's enough to represent the immense talent on a local level.

Hence the Hidden Sussex anthology was born.

I read somewhere on Twitter 'All art is political'. I disagree. All art can be political. This book is political – it sets out to make a positive difference for people of colour (BAME, BME, Black and so on) in Sussex.

It is through all of our continued work as a community – thinking, writing, talking to one another and everyday activism – that we will create and define spaces of our own, where people of colour are at front and centre.

Enjoy the anthology, and please share it with others. #EverydayExcellence #ExtraordinaryExcellence #CreativeCase

Amy Zamarripa Solis
Chair, Writing Our Legacy
@BHwritinglegacy

Acknowledgements

Thank you to all of the people and organisations who made the Hidden Sussex anthology possible.

The contributors: Georgina Aboud, Jenny Arach, Sheila Auguste, Alinah Azadeh, Priti Barua, Bebb Burchell, Josef Cabey, Suchi Chatterjee, Lisa Climie, Joyoti Grech Cato, Sally-Claire Fadelle, Josephine Hall, Jasmine Harris, Maggie Harris, L Oluwafemi Hughes Jonas, Farah Edwards Khan, Dulani Kulasinghe, Georgina Parke, Annie Richardson, Zaid S Sethi, Hayat Nezameddin Shehab, Sonny Singh and Nina Thaddeus.

Editorial Board: Uschi Gatward, Justine Taylor and Amy Zamarripa Solis

Editors: Umi Sinha, Dean Atta and Colin Grant

Artists: Josef Cabey (map) and Jill Carpin (alternative day flag) Ingrid Pollard, *Seaside Series*, 1989.

Hidden Sussex Creative Writing Workshop Leaders: Umi Sinha, Farah Edwards Khan

Writing Our Legacy committee: Bert Williams MBE, Neil Ansell, Graham Lally, Amy Zamarripa Solis

Project partners: Word Factory, New Writing South, Creative Futures, Diversity Lewes, Diverse Crawley, Crawley WORDfest, Shoreham Wordfest, African Night Fever and Brighton & Hove Black History.

Funders: Arts Council England, Brighton & Hove City Council, East Sussex Arts Partnership and Devonshire West Big Local

A special thanks to several people who gave me specialist advice: writer Sean Catt, Lesley from New Writing South, Matt from Creative Futures, and the invaluable book expertise from our Editorial Board, Uschi and Justine.

Last but not least, thank you to British artist and photographer Ingrid Pollard. Ingrid has kindly let us use her art works from her *Seaside Series* (1989) in our anthology.

The works are hand tinted silver prints, text and 3D objects approximately 20 x 24cm in size. They are reminiscent of seaside holiday postcards, illustrating selected souvenirs, such as rock candy and beer steins, and personal photographs.

The *Seaside Series* speaks broadly about tourism, migration and conquest, examining Hastings as a point of departure – or invasion (Battle of 1066). People coming in from Normandy, London, or elsewhere – or going out.

We hope that these art works help you, the reader, think about your relationship to Sussex, with all its complexities, people and history, and deepen the conversation as we look at the past and here-and-now and gaze into the future.

We are grateful that artists, writers, thinkers and activists, such as Ingrid, continue to make interesting, compelling art today.

SUSSEX IN REMEMBRANCE

Suchi Chatterjee
TERRACOTTA CUPS, 1857-1947

Terracotta clay
Moulded by dead hands
In the shadow of Fort William
You bite the bullet
And bitter blood fills your mouth

Cardamoms and ginger
Milk from the gods
Cinnamon on your tongue
Sugar to enthral you

Finger and thumb marks in clay
For a tainted palette
Freedom is a weapon of war
Wrapped in paper cartridges

History is a tattoo
Where is the ritual?
The altered history?
Of a forgotten queen's funeral pyre?

Independence denied
The Black Hole of Calcutta revered
Only Irish voices rebel
Against the profanity of Kipling

In Sussex a fire rages
High on the Downs
Sleeping warriors under a blanket of ash
And a stone pillow for their brothers in arms

The men in the turbans: bows low
It Ain't Half Hot Mum
Screwing the sacred for Empire
The ending is the partition of souls

Walk ankle deep in blood
Mother Gunga falls from the sky
These are our shared tears
Muslim, Hindu, Sikh, Jew, Christian
As we all drink chai from terracotta cup.

Dulani Kulasinghe
ONE LESSON

My first visit to the Chattri was by accident. I had actually gone to the site to see *C-Curve*, a sculpture by Anish Kapoor, installed there for Brighton Festival 2009. The sculpture – a smooth curved mirror that turned the landscape upside down – stood on the side of a green hill, the sky above a clear bright blue. I was a new mother carrying my daughter in a sling. She was interested in her reflection, and we played with seeing ourselves upright and upside down. But I don't remember seeing the Chattri. I think someone – my husband? our Sri Lankan friend studying at Sussex? - mentioned it, but it didn't register, and I have no mental image of it from that sunny day on the Downs. Our attention was focused elsewhere.

Sometimes – often, with Black, Asian and mixed ethnicity history – stories are hidden in plain sight. Built in 1921 on the South Downs, the Chattri sits on the cremation site of 53 Indian soldiers who were injured while serving with British forces in World War I and later died in military hospitals housed in the Royal Pavilion, the Dome, Corn Exchange and York Place. Of that 53, eighteen were treated in the Royal Pavilion and 10 were cremated on the *ghat* or funeral pyre commemorated by the Chattri.

This was my first encounter with the Chattri but it is not unknown in Brighton. Thanks to the Brighton & Hove Black History team and the work of the Chattri Memorial Group, the legacy that the Chattri is built on has been painstakingly researched, illustrated with photographs from the Imperial War Museum and Brighton Museum and is freely available online for anyone who wants to know about it. But who wants to know?

This is a live question for me, because I did not recognise the value of such a legacy until I had children of my own. Until then, I had no reason to contact MOSAIC, a local organisation established over 20 years ago to support Black, Asian and mixed parentage families. But when our older daughter was born and we began attending MOSAIC's precious under-5s playgroup, I found solace for an emptiness I did not fully realise I carried.

Growing up in New Mexico, I was in a minority but still a brown person among brown people; in Brighton I felt alone as a person of colour. But seeing these beautiful children playing around their relaxed, laughing mothers brought home the fundamental importance of having a space in the world where we belong. For those few hours on a Tuesday morning, we did not have to explain our families or steel ourselves against curious looks. At the time, I felt relief. Looking back, I am flooded with gratitude.

Having my own children underscored the profound need for everyone to be aware of the legacy of people of colour in the UK. We remember what matters to us. And if we are all to feel that we matter, and the UK is truly our home, then the stories we tell about the past we must include everyone who played a part. I feel this urgently now in part because my children are at school, learning a British history that I feel must reflect them, but also because the social and political changes happening around us have made it imperative that we all see all of us as active participants in that history.

I work at a school located less than two miles from the Chattri in a Year 2 classroom. The national curriculum for Year 2 includes history, and like every class year, our students are introduced to the Great War. Later, they will also visit the Royal Pavilion in Brighton. In the 100th anniversary year of the Armistice, this carried a particular weight, and the teacher showed a powerpoint to the class in the week before Remembrance Sunday. The children saw a series of black and white photos of soldiers from the Great War and colour photos of elderly white men in uniform wearing medals, with a few references to World War I memorials I did not recognise. Every slide was wreathed in poppies and the slides ended with the phrase, 'Lest we forget.'

I felt deeply uncomfortable sitting there watching and, even worse, listening to the children afterwards. In the way that children do, they personalised what they had just seen, connecting their lives and families to those words and images. It was noticeable that the four children of colour did not participate in the conversation, maybe seeing no reflection of themselves or their families in the slideshow.

Watching them not speak, I was reminded of how, as a child growing up in a middle-class American suburb, I imagined myself into other people's stories and was then surprised at my reflection in the mirror – how is that me, when my imagined me is so… white? It was unbearable to see it play out before my eyes.

I was also mystified that the Chattri – within sight of the homes of some of our students, whose image is the logo for the local high school – was not mentioned once, nor any connection made with the Pavilion. So with the encouragement of the class teacher, who was mortified at this blind spot in the school's teaching material, I made a slideshow of my own.

I had done some research over the summer as part of a volunteer team finding out about the Caribbean and Indian presence along the South Coast during World War I. What I found clarified the radical need for Black History legacy work.

I had not realised that at the start of the war, Britain was badly outnumbered and enlisted the help of battle-ready Indian troops to fight alongside British troops in France – so many that, by September 1914, a third of the British Expeditionary Force stationed in France was Indian.

Over half a million Indian soldiers, 20,000 Caribbean soldiers, 80,000 African soldiers and 92,000 Chinese labourers supported the British war effort during World War I.

Despite living in Brighton for 17 years, visiting the Pavilion, Dome and Corn Exchange regularly, and walking on the Downs most weekends, I did not fully appreciate this history, did not know how many colonised people had been in the UK, in the eastern Mediterranean, on the Western Front, in Palestine, wearing those uniforms, doing that work, fighting in a war that had nothing to do with their own lives.

Finding archives of photographs, official forms and letters documenting the lived experience of people who looked like me, like my Black and Asian friends, transformed my perception of what it means to be British.

The school embraced my slideshow, and all three Year 2 classes saw it. It was very simple and mainly intended to expose a young, largely monocultural group of children to the idea that Britain has historically included people of colour; I also hoped to give children from other backgrounds the feeling that they and their families were not alone here.

But it piqued a few tricky questions, notably, 'Why did they come and fight?' I also had a wonderful conversation with one teacher, who acknowledged his white skin privilege and the 'insularity' of his Catholic school education. Like other teachers I spoke to, he had not known about the extent of the Black and Asian presence in Brighton's history but was glad to know it now and have the material in the classroom.

I last walked out to the Chattri in late October 2018. In the months leading up to that grey Sunday, poppies seemed to be on every lapel – in life, on politicians and TV presenters, on hoardings and school displays. Everywhere it felt as if a steady sombre gaze were focused on 1918, mourning the dead of the Great War as if they had just left the living. There was a freshness to this grief, renewed annually, that in this centenary year seemed to bring the dead closer than ever. Primed by this public mourning of these soldiers – and newly awake to the largely hidden Black and Asian presence in their ranks – the gravity of the Chattri as a memorial finally pulled me in. With a grief as sharp as if for someone I knew, the inadequacy of mere names engraved in marble struck me hard.

But there was also a fitting resonance to the isolated beauty of this strange monument, high on its green hill, with the cold sea wind whipping tears from my eyes, as far from the lives of the men cremated here as it could be. I did not fully pay attention to this legacy before – I did not feel its personal, social, political significance. I have pieced together what little I know over the time I have lived in Brighton, spurred by the experience of becoming a mother and returning to teaching.

The legacy of the Chattri is not simple: it is a single monument to a few men, with no reflection of the diversity of backgrounds and experiences of the many other men who travelled to the UK from throughout the colonies to serve in World War I. There is little public acknowledgement here or elsewhere in Sussex of the Caribbean war dead, the Seaford training camps for colonial troops, or the sinking of the South African troop ship, the SS Mendi, off the Isle of Wight. But even a little knowledge, a few pictures, can make a space for us – however incomplete, that knowing helps us straighten up and find a wider view of this place and ours in it. Seeing ourselves in the world is crucial; public commemorations are significant in how they bury themselves in our and our children's minds, connecting public and private, life and grief. We remember what matters to us.

The Chattri memorialises the moment when the bodies of 53 men passed through a final fire to become and became ash, wind and water. Maybe it also gestures beyond these men to those untold others. Perhaps Kapoor's *C-Curve*, in its temporary, elemental embrace of the changing light of the Downs and sky, reflected this impermanence in ways the Chattri, fraught and incomplete, could not and cannot.

Connecting the story of the Chattri to the story of Brighton's war history is central to a common history that includes us all. We do not have to make it up – it exists already. But we have to *see* it, embodied in the Chattri and the use of the Pavilion as a military hospital, in the mossy Commonwealth war graves all around Sussex, and illuminated on the internet in the work of the groups mentioned above as well as national institutions like the Imperial War Museum. We must embed this history into how we view the present so that we may fully feel that we belong, not only within the walls of a playgroup, but in the world we all inhabit.My own awareness of my place in the world is partial and shifting, but the more I see our experiences reflected in the stories around me, the more at ease I feel. Though the poppies are gone and the fanfare and funding cycles to memorialise the centenary of the so-called Great War have ceased, the solidity of the Chattri is a reassuring, grounding reminder of my own place within these green and lovely hills that are now my home.

EAST SUSSEX

Maggie Harris
PULLING INTO RYE BY TRAIN

Ready for the shops, cobbled streets, Mermaid Street,
lunch at the cheapest pub we could find. Somewhere in our consciousness,
this was Olde England. This was what we'd been promised through movies
and postcards, magazines of *Country Life*. We staggered on the cobbles,
arched our necks at posh old houses, their black and white beams, posed
by red telephone boxes, enjoyed the feeling of being somewhere *different*.
These were the days before pound shops. Instead, collectables
attracted, ceramics from the pottery. Copper and glass and architectural
salvage we only skimmed, you couldn't take those on the train.
We never bought much, though a teacup or two found its way into Mum's bag,
turning up at Christmas with a note in her best convent school writing,
 'You liked this in Rye, remember?'
The exception was that second-hand shop
 (*vintage* now) by The Windmill,
full of haute couture. We bought bundles then: frocks
and bags and shoes. And in the barn by the station,
my tie-dyed maxi-dress, watermarked
peppermint green: it would dance at African workshops, stretch for babies,
appear at folk festivals.
Thirty years later, it's just started to split at the seams.

Lisa Climie
MY MOTHER SAID

My mother said, I never should
Play with the gypsies in the wood.
If I did, she would say;
'Naughty girl to disobey!'
                    - English children's song

Being outsiders in a rural community was a challenge, but my parents rose to it well. I was very young when we moved with my paternal grandmother, Kit, who suffered from early stage dementia, from Brighton to Kingsdown, a remote Tudor farmhouse in East Sussex.

Normally my encounters with Kit were brief and argumentative; for some reason I gained an odd pleasure from taking the contrary view to hers. We'd had one of these little exchanges recently while watching Hattie Jacques and Eric Sykes on the television.

'She doesn't get any thinner, does she?' Kit said, referring to Hattie.

'Yes she does,' I replied.

I could see my mother trying not to laugh as she threw me a half-hearted scolding stare.

'Isn't it her bedtime yet?' said Kit, annoyingly, because I thought that if I kept a low enough profile everyone would forget about bedtime and I would get to stay up with the grown-ups and watch telly.

A sure way of getting a rise out of Kit was to lie on the sofa that ran along the back wall of the sitting room, walking my feet up and down the wattle and daub plaster between the dark oak beams while hanging my head off the seat of the sofa. I liked the feeling of the cool lumpy wall beneath my feet. It wouldn't take long for Kit to notice and we would then have our usual exchange.

'I really don't think you should have your feet on that wall.'

'Why not?'

'Because you will knock the plaster down and make dirty marks with your feet.'

'No I won't.'

My debating skills were not yet honed, so this was the best I could come up with. After a few more rounds of this circular argument, I would remove my feet. Then when Kit was settled, I would put them up again.

I remember my early childhood as a happy time running wild about the farm, the surrounding fields and woods. Totally tomboy, I dressed in shorts and T-shirts in warm weather, and jeans, jumpers and wellington boots on colder, wetter days. Apart from school uniform, skirts and dresses were not part of my wardrobe.

The children's song, 'My Mother Said', gives some sense of the attitudes of the time, although the complete opposite was true of my mother as she would actively have encouraged me playing in the woods with gypsies had the opportunity arisen. She championed outsiders and misfits and was forever filling the house with the human equivalent of stray dogs.

One such person, Marty Cairncross-Lee, was from a gypsy family and, being a known rascal, attracted attention from the police when there was any local misdemeanour. At one point, Marty found himself homeless with his wife, Sybil, eight months pregnant. Mum took them in. It was only a few days later, at six in the morning, that the police raided our house looking for Marty. They stormed in on him and Sybil as they slept in the end bedroom of our old farmhouse.

I ran in from my bedroom next door, which I shared with my brother Simon, to see what all the commotion was, just as Mum rounded on Dave Carter, the local bobby. With a flick of her head, the deep auburn fringe that covered her right eye flew back, allowing both pale blue eyes to fix on the now nervous-looking policeman.

'Jesus Christ, Dave, did you have to bring the heavy mob? Could you not have telephoned or come at a decent hour?' Dave Carter, a bit out of his depth, muttered, 'They said he would do a runner if he was tipped off.'

'Bloody hell, Dave, he's not Al Capone. We'll see about this.'

I knew that tone well and it meant he was definitely in trouble.

'Don't you go anywhere till I get dressed.'

With that, she turned and left the room. I noticed she was wearing Dad's favourite paisley-patterned silk dressing gown and a pair of wellington boots.

Simon had now joined me in the doorway, and as Mum stomped past we looked at each other and then back into the room as Sybil, who was sitting on the edge of the bed in her long floral nightie, cried out in a shrill voice, 'It's started, Marty, it's started!' Then to PC Carter she wailed, 'You've brought the baby on, that's what you've done.'

Marty was cursing as the police, having told him to 'get some clothes on' manhandled him out of the room.

'Get your filthy 'ands off me, you f***ing pigs. It's a bloody stitch-up. Can't you lot think of anyone else to arrest?'

Marty's words trailed behind him as he disappeared down the small back staircase in the corner of the room.

Dave Carter seemed to hesitate before following, no doubt worried he would feel more of my mother's wrath for not doing as she had asked.

Me? Well, I found it very exciting and wondered if the drama meant a day off school.

Elements of what happened at our house with Marty would later be played out at my village school when some Romany children, whose family had camped locally, were enrolled there for a short time. Tyso and his kin were the only encounter I had with anyone from a different racial background, apart from Marty and Sybil.

Our small farming community seemed to be entirely white, though I was aware from television that this wasn't the case everywhere in the world because TV newscasters often talked of a place called Rhodesia, where a white man called Ian Smith, who spoke with a very odd accent, constantly talked about coloured people. I imagined them to be red and blue and green, failing to make the connection with the comments about me: 'She's got a touch of the tar brush, hasn't she?' I supposed that being likened to a tar brush was one up from being called a loo brush because at least a tar brush wouldn't have been stuck down a lavatory. My parents had told me the nurses at Brighton hospital had joked that I looked like a loo brush at birth, because of my mass of black hair.
From the beginning, Tyso and his younger brother were distrusted and faced active aggression from pupils and

teachers alike. Tyso – who, like me, was eight – spent most of playtime fighting other boys to defend himself and his brother. When not being attacked, the two were isolated and ignored.

Being a person who felt always alone, even when with others, I sensed a connection with this boy and wanted to be his friend, although initially I was not brave enough to speak to him.

Soon the unpleasantness towards them grew. Things started to go missing from people's satchels, and the culprits could only be the gypsy boys, of course. I knew this was not true; that others were stealing and blaming them because they thought they could get away with anything while Tyso and his brother would get the blame.

It was then that I found the courage to speak to Tyso. I had learnt from my mother's example to stand up for underdogs, the different and the victimised, a lesson that has never left me. My support didn't make any difference to the outcome, though, since shortly after that Tyso and his family moved on.

The culture of prejudice experienced by Tyso and his brother flowed from the top down at our school. Headmaster Baxter, known to all as Bully Baxter or Baxter the Beast, scared me so much that even seeing the producer's name at the end of Blue Peter – 'Biddy Baxter' – would give me the heebie-jeebies.

Our own Baxter never picked on anyone his own size. From a distance of 50 years, I remember him vividly as a giant of a man. Although this may have more to do with my size while attending his primary school than the reality. My recollection is that of a tall and broad-shouldered man with greased-back greying hair combed into ridges like corrugated iron. He had a perpetually angry red face, and a deep, booming voice. He was the thing of nightmares for me, the giant at the top of a beanstalk that I must hack and hack away at to prevent him climbing down.

Fortunately, I was not on Baxter's radar, being too young and insignificant. When I first joined the school, aged four, I was in the relative safety of the infants' class, while my sister Sarah, six years my senior, had to brave the slipper-wielding, intolerant and ignorant brute daily.

Baxter had his favourites, whom he rewarded with tasks such as feeding and cleaning out his racing pigeons. These special few would also be hand-picked to pass the 11-plus. Sarah was not one of the chosen ones and would be chided for such heinous crimes as reading a book.

My personal day of dread arrived when I was approaching my ninth birthday, and followed the sudden illness of my form teacher, Miss Cross, a pleasant Mrs Pepperpot-type character, a mild-mannered woman who wore a blouse and a long skirt with her silver hair scraped back in a tight bun. I did wonder if she might shrink at night-time. But tall or small, on this occasion she wasn't there and we were told to our horror that we must join Mr Baxter's class for the day.

I can't remember the course of events that led to him inspecting my neck. It was the start of summer term and the Easter holidays had been blessed with unseasonably hot weather. My hair, as always, was cut short, and my neck, like the other parts of my body exposed to the sun, had turned a deep brown – the colour of the sun-baked conkers that would later drop from our horse chestnut tree, breaking out of their spiky armour to expose their honeyed mahogany skins.

'Maria,' Baxter bellowed from behind my chair to one of his acolytes. 'I have a task for you. Take this girl to the cloakroom and clean her neck.'

Maria grabbed my arm and led me away like a condemned prisoner. As we reached the classroom door, Baxter boomed out again, 'Clean, mind, Maria. Use lots of soap and a nail brush.'

The predominant feeling as she scrubbed my neck was of pure fear, the kind that makes you want to puke and cower, that reaches inside you and grabs the pit of your stomach and holds it in a clenched fist. An overwhelming desire welled up in me to run and keep running. And although every fibre of me knew that what was happening was wrong, my shaky sense of self allowed this experience to leave a deep imprint of shame on me.

Suddenly, I remembered Tyso, and the day he said to me on the bus home from school, 'It's not gypsies that are dirty, it is the Gadjo.'

That day, a small group of older children had followed him to the bus, the leader of the gang egging on others by taunting him with, 'Dirty gypsy.'
Tyso ignored him.

'I said, you dirty gypsy. Can you smell something?' he asked the others.

'Yes, a stinking dirty gypsy,' came the reply.

This had gone on all the way to the bus stop. I kept looking at Tyso, waiting for him to say something, but he didn't until we had got on the bus.

'Who are the Gadjo?' I asked, thinking it might be some sort of animal or a creature from Doctor Who, like the Daleks.

'People who are not gypsies.'

'Hang on a minute! Are you saying I'm dirty, then?'

'Got a lavatory in your house?'

'Yes of course. We have three.'

'Well, that's even worse.'

'Why's that?'

'Because when you pass the rubbish that comes from your body into the lavatory and pull the chain, it travels through your walls in pipes and goes straight past your kitchen where your mother makes your food,' he said.

He clearly didn't know my mother!

'Well, what do you do with your – er – rubbish?' I felt slightly annoyed now.

'I dig a hole for it. My mother is so particular about cleanliness that even if the edge of one of her best plates – the ones with the pictures of horses on – gets a little chip, she will break it and throw it out, because it will never be clean.'

In the clutches of Maria that day, I would rather have been a full-blood Romany than a Gadgo. They seemed much nicer people. Now I wonder if this was how Tyso felt when the other children tormented him for being darker, different. I will never know, as I wouldn't see Tyso, Baxter or Maria ever again.

The thought of Baxter even now makes me want to seek out his grave and jump up and down on it like a demented banshee. It would change nothing, but I might feel a little better.

The person who rescued me was Mum. Upon hearing what happened, she was immediately on the warpath. As my father would say of her, years later, 'She took no prisoners.' Whatever demons from her own past spurred her on, Sarah, Simon and I always knew that she would fight to the death for us. We also knew we didn't want to be on the receiving end of her ferocious temper. When she blew, we flew, especially if she was wielding a cattle stick. We all learnt to run fast and scatter to a number of outdoor hideaways until things calmed down.

I don't know exactly what Mum said to Baxter. I think she may have threatened him with a visit from Carter, perhaps feeling he still owed her one from the Marty fiasco. Whatever she did, Simon and I were immediately removed from the school. Within a week we were installed into the very calm environment of another village primary instead. This was only a short distance from the secondary modern where Sarah, at 15, was enrolled, now more interested in boys than books.

Shortly after this, on my ninth birthday, Granny Kit, who in her younger days had been a tailoress, presented me with a rectangular white box. As her dementia had progressed, she had begun to spend more and more time in her bedroom with her precious Singer sewing machine, rarely venturing out.

This day, her gnarled hands thrust the box in my direction from her favourite high-back armchair. 'My dear, it's for you. Many happy returns.'

I reached out hesitantly, surprised she remembered who I was, let alone that it was my birthday.

Inside the white box, wrapped in tissue paper, was a traditional gypsy girl's outfit. It had a little white blouse, a full red skirt and green scarf with what looked like tiny coins sewn around its edge. There was even a red waistcoat with a fringe running along the bottom. This was a disappointing gift, as I had no interest in dressing up in anything remotely girly, although even at nine years old I could appreciate what a beautiful piece of needlework it was. I was still amazed she had given me anything at all.

Dad spotted my confusion about my birthday gift, and taking me aside, explained to me that, like Kit and himself, I was part Romany. He told me that when he was younger, Kit would read his cards and tea leaves and tell his fortune. These skills, he said, were only ever passed on to the girls in gypsy families, so as an only child he had not been taught them. I would be the next in line to receive these special gifts. The dressing-up outfit was a symbol of this.

I still wasn't keen to wear a dress, but my grandmother instantly become a much more interesting and exotic person to me as I wondered where exactly she kept her crystal ball, and if she would pass this on to me, too. From that moment I felt a special bond was forged between us.

Maggie Harris
THE HASTING LINE, AS WAS

As soon as you left Ashford it was a different country,
the train taking its time through cornfield and woodland
field and panoramic sky gliding back into the past,
with stops at Ham Street and Appledore.

We all leaned out, the babies and me, sisters, Mum
remembering steam trains through Demerara,
another life ago, where bananas lined the track.

But here we were now, a ride on the old diesel train
with its slide-down windows and lean-out doors,
its private carriages, its whistle
pulling into Rye,
and we're stepping off, into yet another country.

Annie Richardson
WEAVING THE THREADS

I have a mixed heritage. My father was white and a typical
Sussex man who 'won't be druv'. My mother is black. My cloth
is cut from the fabric of both black and white. I don't want to
deny the white part of me. I am very proud of being born in
Sussex, and I love many things from the quirky culture of East
Sussex that have made me who I am. However, that part of
me isn't the obvious part to others who don't know me. It is
not the part of me that others see when they look at me.
Often it is not the part that they want to know about.

I am slightly fed-up that even in 2019, I still have the
following conversation:

'Where are you from?'

'I'm from East Sussex.'

'No, I mean before. You know where do you COME
from?'

'Yep, East Sussex. I was born in East Sussex.'

'Oh ok…but are you Caribbean, or African?'

That, in a nutshell, is the source of my disquiet. I am, as
I said, cut from the cloth of both black and white, and I have
stitched for myself an identity since my birth. My 57-year-old
suit has been sown as a patchwork: from the ways that people

have made me feel about myself. I have internalised the positive and negative experiences into a view of myself and my worth and used this in my decisions on how I respond to, and form relationships with others. Most of the time I quite like and am proud of the suit I have sown, but sadly others keep picking at the seams.

My mum came to East Sussex in the 1950s aged 16 from a tiny island which is part of the British Overseas Territories. She did not speak much of her home when I was small. I now wonder if that was partly because she had shut off those memories for fear of the pain caused by leaving behind her beloved mum and home that was too far away to visit. When people questioned my mum's background and asked if she came from the Caribbean or Africa she would say loudly that she was British and from a small island owned by Great Britain.

Looking back now, I realise how strongly she held onto this in order to prove she had a right to live in Britain even though she was a different colour. I realise that in some ways she was more quintessentially British than many. She had been brought up with very British traditions that had hung on from a colonial past. Pictures of the Royal family and the Union Jack were everywhere and schools taught British history. I often think she was more patriotic and more entrenched in Britishness than some in our rural village. The island seems always to have been described as like going back in time, and visitors enjoy that. My mum was slightly embarrassed by what she saw as some of the more backward traditions, and their lack of modern facilities and material things when she was growing up and wouldn't often be drawn into talking of it. The

Islanders have a particular dialect, but by the time I was old enough to talk, my mother spoke with a near-perfect soft BBC British accent.

I now realise how much this was her armour against the slurs that she should 'go back' to where she came from. She lived in a very small village where she had the only black face and was married to a white man: something which was taboo in the 1950s. It took a long time to be accepted. She found ways to 'fit in' and to be the same rather than different, and to an extent leave behind who she was on an island hundreds of miles away. I now realise that what saved her from sinking, left me adrift in terms of my identity. I had no culture to align myself to. I now understand that coming from a colonised island had stripped her of a culture, other than the one that was fed to its people on a plate by its masters.

In much later years I have researched my ancestry and found my maternal lineage was from Africa, brought to the island as slaves. I excitedly told my mum who smiled and changed the subject. What I was proud to declare, she seemed embarrassed by. My mum did not see herself as from Africa – her patchwork suit was made-up from her island identity and 'Britishness'. When she came to Britain alone and so obviously 'other' but trying to fit in, she held out to those that sometimes shirked her what she felt would make her accepted – the British part. She was just responding to them picking at the seams.

I was a Sussex girl but did not look like one. I had a round, brown, smiley face and a mass of frizzy black hair, which when I was small my mum would pull into submission until the tears came to my eyes. I had a thick bottom lip that I would stick out when I was sulking, and my dad would say 'wind'll change and you'll stay like that'. He would say it with affection as he ruffled my hair, but others would pick out that facial feature as a source of derision. When I was small, and we went out my mum would give me a spit wash: face, elbows and knees. When I squirmed and protested she would say 'no one will say we are dirty' – the slur that she had heard too often on her arrival in England.

Being one of the only black faces at primary school wasn't easy. I had a rather idyllic life at home and it wasn't until I went to school that the fact that as a family we were different really hit me. All my friends were white. I have a strong memory of coming home from primary school, crying to my mum that I wanted to be white like my friends and that I was upset by the name calling. She smiled and hugged me saying 'You can't change that. Choose your battles. Often it is better to ignore it and just walk away. Be a friend. Be good.' And there it was: her view that this was the best way to be accepted, or at least that is what my young brain heard and internalised.

For many years it shaped how I approached the world. Smile and laugh. Please people. Try and make everyone like you by being fun and bright and good. Don't rock the boat, fit in. When 'jokes' were made, such as 'Don't give me that black look', I learned to smile and ignore the sharp painful twist in my tummy. I learned to believe the words: 'It's only a joke. I don't see you as black.' I learned to deny my blackness; there were no allies, no friends who looked like me. I learned that sometimes it was simpler to take the sting out of their 'jokes' by saying those things first.

Despite my mum's words, I tried to be like my white friends. My favourite early play was to put a petticoat on my head and pretend I had long straight hair like them. I would pretend to brush it and toss my waving petticoat-hair around like they did. Occasionally, I raised my eyes to look for people that looked like me. My parents' Sunday paper recorded the crimes committed by black people, but there was seldom anything positive. The books I read at school showed smiling, red-lipped, rosy-cheeked white children, but none like me. My mum and dad would watch *The Black and White Minstrel Show*, and I remember wondering why this entertained them. The black part of my patchwork identity was small and frayed because my experiences of living where I did had picked at the seams.

My hair has featured significantly in shaping my identity, causing confusion in my teenage life. When I was 12, Mum decided to take me to a hairdresser's to have my hair 'tidied up'. I begged her for an Afro as I had begun to see black people with this hairstyle on *Top of the Pops* and in my sister's *Jackie* magazine. Taking me to the hairdressers meant getting on a train to London. There were no hairdresser's close to home that would know what to do with my unruly frizz or look at it without hiding their horror. When I got off the train, I remember being amazed at the brown faces. Instead of being pleased at seeing people like me, I was frightened. These people weren't like me, were they? They were loud, laughing and confident, many with an accent I couldn't understand. What were these people to me?

We arrived at the hairdresser's and I walked into a new world which I would visit often over the next 20+ years. A black hairdresser's shop then, was nothing like a white hairdresser. The first thing that hit me was the heat, the chemical smell, the noise and the pounding beat of reggae – oh, I loved the music. There were women of every shade from light brown to ebony black. The customers were sat laughing and fast-talking with the ladies who stood behind them, combs held in greased hands. There were customers with heads tilted back over sinks, while younger apprentices washed, lathered and massaged their heads of curly hair. Other women sat under noisy hairdryers, peering out through the plastic visors, all with big curlers covered by black cloths – the slight acrid smell of singed hair and chemical. Sweat dripping down their faces, some signalled to the young apprentices 'am I done yet, girl?' and as my mum and I entered that space, all eyes swivelled suspiciously towards us.

My mum explained to the girl on the desk that she was there for 'a straighten' and pointed to me with rolling eyes 'and my daughter wants an Afro'. I remember sitting in that special hairdresser's chair – looking in the mirror at the different world I was suddenly inhabiting, which was so alien to my world and my little white village.

A beautiful black woman stood behind me with straightened hair cut perfectly into coiffured loveliness. She said something to me that I couldn't understand. I stuttered, 'Pardon me?' She looked at me as if I was slow or stupid and repeated slowly, 'Why you want a 'fro girl? Why not have a straighten like you mudda?'

I must have looked like a rabbit in the headlights because my mum, who was sitting in the chair next to mine, said, 'Maybe next time...she's just having an Afro cut today.' The beautiful black woman let out an audible 'tsk' through her teeth, signalled to a young girl, who I followed to a sink for a hair wash. This was a lesson – black women at that time usually had their hair straightened. This involved harsh chemicals, which if left on too long left nasty weeping burns. For many years to come I succumbed to my frizz being tamed and straightened. Or I had extensions added to my own hair with a long day of plaiting to get a similar effect of hair-tossing and waving as my petticoat hair. It may not be the same for others, but for me this painful transformation was so that I could have hair more like my white friends and acceptable to where I lived. I was informed at school that it was definitely better to have 'neat' hair as I was more likely to get a job. It wasn't until my forties that I embraced my own hair and what it meant to my black identity.

The beautiful black hairdresser started to rake a comb through my tangled frizz. As I sat there, my stupidity temporarily forgotten, the beautiful black woman said, 'And where you from?'

'I'm from a little village in East Sussex,' adding when I saw her confused face 'near Brighton?' After all everyone knew Brighton, didn't they?

'Nah, I mean you Caribbean or African?'

And there it was again. I had thought this question was only asked of me by white people, but I have found that it comes from black people too, but for different reasons. For black people it's about seeking a shared past. The problem for me was that I didn't know what my background was at that time. In my head I was neither, and in my experience, and in my patchwork-identity I was more white than black. At this point in my life, once again the seams were unpicked but this time by people I thought were more the same as me.

From that moment forwards, I felt, as my mum says, neither fish nor fowl. I stuttered at that beautiful woman a story of a small island in the middle of the Atlantic Ocean, volcanic, owned by Britain. She nodded distractedly and turned away, which was a relief. It freed me to listen, as I did over the years that followed, to the lilt of the foreign-to-me accents, the laughter, the music, the discussions of costumes for carnival, relatives at home, food, clothes... all things that marked their culture. For many years, this culture made me feel like 'other', with the only thing that we shared being the colour of our skin and the abuse we suffered because of that.

I returned to school proudly wearing a pair of wedge shoes borrowed from my sister underneath a perfectly round Afro. My dear friend says she still remembers that day, she felt like I had changed over the summer holidays into someone different.

Perhaps I had changed as I realised that there was possibly a different way of being if you were black than the habits I had formed. It didn't last – much like my Afro after the first heavy rainfall. I walked back into my comfortable way of being – laughing, joking, denying, walking away. Friends crowded around my new hair, patting and stroking, and we laughingly took all the pencils from my pencil case and pushed them in my big hair one by one.

When I was about 15 a young (white) new deputy-head stepped in to take a lesson when a teacher was absent. He asked us to describe ourselves. I had picked up the language of the day and described myself as coloured. He appeared annoyed: 'Green? Blue? No, you are black, and you should be proud of that – black people have fought hard to be recognised equally in society.' I was angry. In my head black wasn't something to be proud of, and he had drawn attention to my difference in front of the whole class.

I shouted back at him, 'You're white! What do you know? I can call myself what I want to – it's my decision', immediately shocked at myself for raising my voice at a teacher and waited for my punishment.

He smiled at me like he'd won something. 'Yes, you can. Remember that.'

I now realise that this was a point which started the weaving back together of my identity – a re-forming of my patchwork. I can't say I walked out of there being anything but angry and embarrassed. No one talked about my colour. That was the bit that I kept under-wraps – I had learned from my mum that you had to fit in, not draw attention to your difference, not complain, not mention racism.

White people I met over the years after I left school often said, 'Things have got better though, haven't they – there's not as much prejudice or racism is there?' From their position this was probably true, but from my position the answer was different, even though I nodded my agreement so as not to make them feel bad. The abuse from a passing car; the 'friendly banter' with racist undertones; the complaints that people are 'pulling the race card'; the 'reassurance – 'you know I didn't mean you'; the flat that mysteriously stopped being available in between the phone call and the viewing and on seeing the colour of my skin; the stepping in front of me in a queue with the look that said 'and what will *you* do about it'; all of those small regular happenings marked me as 'other'.

What that teacher had done for me was to make me think. Each experience, everything I read or watched that made me notice my difference, helped me to position myself and who I was, because I was at last aware that I had some sort of choice. A choice that was to a degree denied to my mother in her quest to fit in. Each time I noticed and decided, I wove together the threads of my frayed identity.

I have spent the years since then trying to weave the threads together and understand my roots, because it matters. Having a better sense of who I am has helped me feel more able to challenge the 'banter', the jokes, the injustices, and say, 'Whatever your intention, this is not OK.'

Words matter. There is so much to do to try to weed out the deficit language, the assumptions, the deterministic views, the tendency to homogenise people into 'they'. Much more needs to be done for all people who are 'other' to see themselves reflected in the spaces they inhabit, for without that how can they even begin to weave together the threads? I know for certain I am a black woman born in East Sussex and I won't be druv.

Joyoti Grech Cato
WHITEHAWK WOMAN AT CUCKMERE HAVEN

Standing lookout on the brow of the hill, the sheep sleeping under gorse that burns bright with yellow flowers in daylight, dark at night now with all of us asleep, I am awake.

Deeply rooted in this island, yet some white magic rolls over invisible generation after generation, and every generation digs to rediscover ourselves over and over again.

Held in the spiralling embrace of time and land, draped in the wrap of heavy sea mist that rises from the water and drifts inland, so far, I persist.

Looking down from my standpoint, I see the silver river serpent its way slowly, meandering across the marshes. More than once, I was the fog, rolling inland as I rose from the saltwater marshes, and more than once, the flint farmhouse, and much later, the furrowed field in winter.

They said I was brave when I walked out into the field, until I lost the farmhouse. It wasn't brave. I was held by the dark path at my feet when I looked down, and then, in the instant the farmhouse disappeared by the fog that set me free. Spirit in all things, my siblings surrounded me. Not fearful, not brave.

All the human ties that bound me disappeared, and the land reclaimed me, and I returned into its love. The mother and lifesaver, the blood and bone and marrow, the earth matched by my skin, the sea by my eyes, the winds by the soft cloud of my hair and whispering in my breath and spirit.

I have always been here.

This generation of me is recently arrived but my family sees in you and me, the face we seem to share.

Our family, living so close in geographical space, from Whitehawk Enclosure to Eastern Road, to the place where the river rolls its double question mark down to the wider waters of the sea haven.

Time draws us through its kaleidoscope, Neolithic to the closing moments of the Anthropocene era. Some of us have been signalling the extinction to each other across water and land, from Furamon to Standing Rock, in extending circles that finally are spiralling outwards.

Since I walked here with the People, we have always been here. We watched the great green smooth skin and scales evolve to feathers and then the early murmurations swoop and whirl in the wide red sky.

We were strong when we set off, the curious ones, determined, the outcasts and explorers. The arrowhead, the cutting edge.

We did not say we helped each other. There was no other. We walked together, and we carried those who could not. We fed ourselves with the wild *za'atar* that grew in profusion along the way, and the *lawza* although it was *vitkadhira* when we brought it with us, and its perfume was protection potent enough to keep away hostilities, at least from those with two legs and a sense of smell.

We brought change as we passed through, wittingly and innocently both. Animal life shape-shifted, lifted its wings, entered into unfamiliar element and made there its home. Herb and shrub transformed, flowering at our fetid season, scattering seed in our infants' playthings with songs and laughter, teasing and tears, and left behind in our remains.

Accompanying our movement, the earth moved also and the waters broke in an eruption of continental re-formation. The South bestowed upon the North its gift of brilliant cliffs. The ancient sisters split apart, all four A's beginning and ending our names. Asia and Africa even though still linked, now surrounded by seas and Seven new Sisters rose up at the edge of the land where we settled. Although we walked here, if ever any one of our exhausted sleeps threw up nightmares of unsafe return, now that journey would take a vessel, or strong swimmers, or surrender to the whim of the water.

We have always been here.

In Mothertongue there is no singular I. The way we speak the earth and its life into being has only a First People, no first person, of any verb.

Time - circular, spherical, a shape that maybe has no name, is hidden in these words.

Time is always.

Now living a short walk from our original home, that is itself a long walk from our aboriginal home, we are history in progress. We are the fog and the farmhouse and the furrowed field.

Maggie Harris
OF WORDS

My cousin from Trinidad tossing her black hair over the bar in Lewes,
tagging along with us poets, not trusting the word 'workshop',
unable to extinguish the image of her husband wiping his hands on oilcloths
in the garage, back in Arima. But all of these words are strange:
Fulking, Clymping, Hammer Bottom, Cuckfield.
Dial Post makes her giggle, and we're talking about the mail and how letters
never reach her unless addressed to a mother-in-law in the next town,
Mrs. Don't-Mess-with-me-Invincible.

'Imagine you a poet, *you*,' she laughs, and we're
remembering
that one black and white photo circa 1963:
us frozen on the swing in the backyard,
as if we're back there still, waiting for a push.

Farah Edwards Khan
MARTYRS ON PARADE

I didn't want to leave Brighton and go back to India, I just
wanted to spend more time with Tim. The six-month visa was
coming to an end, and plane tickets were booked to fly back
to Bombay. My heart ached, and I couldn't eat or sleep.

Yellow leaves slowly began to fall from weeping trees.
Starlings massed over the old West Pier, which had not yet
been destroyed by fire. Some days had crisp air and golden
sunshine, others were damp and heavy, grey-hued like the
skin of a dying man.

Tim mentioned that Lewes Bonfire night would soon be
bringing about a great public gathering. As a child in Bhopal I
had heard the poem's words: 'Remember, remember, the fifth
of November, the gunpowder treason and plot...'

Instead of the date, I remembered my mother,
exaggerated red lips and eyes stretched-wide in recitation,
between chews of paan. I don't think she ever did explain the
significance of the events the poem named but failed to
describe.

Bonfire night. The public processions I'd joined in India
took place in daylight, I had never walked at sundown. What
kind of remembrance needed the cover of darkness to
express itself?

The narrow streets of Lewes are filled with thick smoke, an orange hue has blanketed the town centre, intoxicated men and women sway on the pavement, laughing and shouting. People dressed in black and white stripes holding up burning crosses and heads on stakes stride jauntily along the road. Life-sized papier-mâché effigies of Guy Fawkes tied up, his head bent low on a cart, bump past, dragged by men dressed in Jacobean costumes and high hats. Many clutch flaming torches that swoosh above the crowd of heads.

My thoughts drift back to when I was about six and my nanny Hasina walked me for what seemed like miles to see the Moharram procession in the old city. 'Chalo, Baby, you must come with me to see all this and learn what it is to love God.' Moharram, I was to learn, was not for the faint-hearted. I watched, dumbstruck, hundreds of distant-eyed men rhythmically slashing at themselves while incanting, mournfully, 'Ya Hussain… Ya Hussain' – drawing welts and bright blood, wielding swords and whips dripping with fresh gore, a thrashing, pounding mass martyrdom trailed by grieving wives, sisters, and mothers. This macabre procession shuffled along bearing tall papier-mâché replicas of mosques and Shia monuments elaborately decorated with gold and silver and carried by men dressed in black. They took turns to lift these heavy burdens to shoulder height in order that those seeking longevity and happiness could pass under them.

In the present, a shatter of magenta fireworks lights up the northern sky. Sulphur fills the nostrils as black metal drums pass by, pulsating, backed by the roar of fires housed in carts that rumble across cobbled stones, throwing sudden fierce heat at the press of onlookers and their awed faces: small children on parent's shoulders, mouths agape at the orgy of noise and incandescence. The wailing of bagpipes grips the heart like a sea siren.

The secret of the seven societies is now out. 'A rope, a rope, to hang the Pope, a penn'orth of cheese to choke him, a pint of beer to wash it down, and a jolly good fire to burn him.' Young and old together tread the parade, which snakes its way through twisting, claustrophobic lanes, a serpentine creature full of jovial pride in the history of England, playfully denouncing the deaths of the 17, whom some faraway Queen commanded be burned at the stake for their beliefs.
In my childhood Bhopal, Moharram's pride blazed with a different intensity.

Above black mourning trousers, shirtless torsos glistened with fresh crimson. Collections of steel swords and spears were borne by these bloodied men in a trance. Some held short chains tipped with metal blades that, as they were rhythmically jerked back over or around shoulders, spread like talons to hack across raw open skin. A burst of shouting urged onlookers to get back out of the way; another half-naked man suddenly emerged, scampering and bucking along past the crowd like a mad horse tied with ropes, as though he were possessed or under a spell. As more warnings were boomed out to 'keep away', the man chanted sounds of a language, which no one could understand. Throughout this spectacle the parade's lamentation, its insistent cadence, drove the flailing remorselessly on.

I had never seen such insanity before. Green and red was everywhere, poison and blood, depicting how the grandsons of the prophet were slain for water. Nobody in the procession smiled; there was no laughter, only grief, as fierce as if the marchers had just heard the awful tidings of 680 AD.

But there were also food stalls with steaming kichara (spicy meat porridge), pakoras, hard boiled eggs served with salt, tandoori chicken on hot skewers and, yes, 'old ladies hair' – or candy floss - which I loved so much.

In Lewes, by the hot dog sellers and the toffee apples, hawkers sell Native American feathers, head dresses with large horns, and swords, moulded in China, that run red only with the timed flashing of led lights. The atmosphere is festive, elated. Perhaps for a child not, after all, so different to the martyrs' remembrance from which Hasina always bought me back home, safe, with a smile on my face and balloon in my hand, stuffed with candy floss and blessed by the bloody spirit of Moharram. But I am not, this time, going happily home. Will this fire, smoke, commotion be my last memory of England?

Josef Cabey
PHEASANTS

Flash, a flash of red, a flash of green, a flash of mottled feathers out there in the fields.

I'm moving, moving through the countryside, sitting on the number 28 bus, travelling between Brighton and Lewes. Riding, I'm riding on a pale yellow bus, a pale yellow bus with details of red.

I used to travel for miles on buses, the bright red double decker buses of my home town London. Number 38, this was my favourite bus. It took me to art school; it took me clubbing in the West End. It took me to all the places I wanted to go. Yes the number 38, the 38 was my favourite bus of all.

I live in Sussex these days, and here I am trundling again between Brighton and Lewes on that yellow and red bus spotting pheasants, spotting pheasants in the fields over yonder, spotting pheasants from the top of the bus. I think of a lasting memory, a memory of spotting pheasants, a memory of spotting pheasants as a child.

I really am a city boy, a London boy born of parents from faraway places.

But sometimes, sometimes I went to the English countryside. In the beginning on school trips, later to visit friends I met through education, friends who came from other UK places, places that meant I had to travel through the countryside, mostly on coaches. Every time I made those journeys, the childhood ones and the adult ones, I was fascinated by those flashes of red, flashes of green, flashes of mottled feathers that meant only one thing: pheasants!

When travelling back then I never really felt that I had arrived in the countryside till I saw my first pheasant. Today I've spotted four. Four male pheasants; I know this because it is only the guys that sport that colour. So in reality, I've always been spotting guys, I guess they are easier to make out. So sitting on that bus, travelling between those two places, I spot the pheasants, and as they have for many years, they make me smile.

It is summer, the sun is shining, and I look out into the fields and spot those flashes of red, those flashes of green, flashes of mottled feathers.

Ah pheasants!

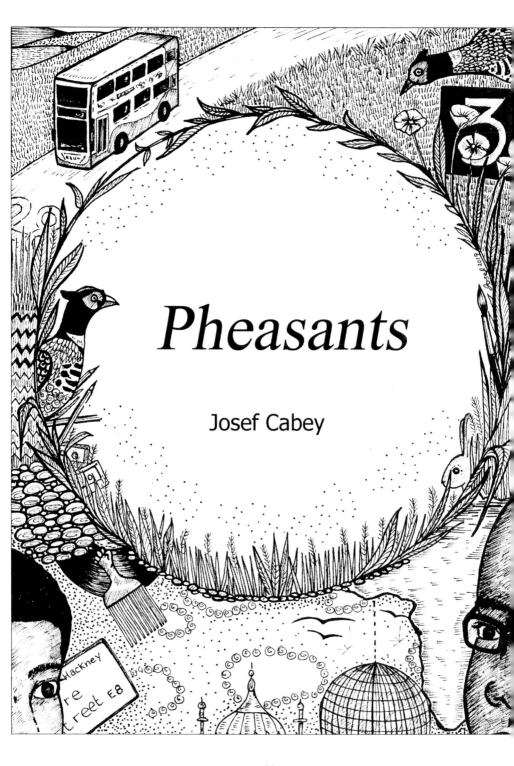

Pheasants

Josef Cabey

Seaside Series (1989)
by Ingrid Pollard

This postcard shows me at the seaside, down for the day. Here's another one of me having a cream tea.

Hastings is at the edge, the boundary, the shoreline. It's the seaside town where everyone comes from somewhere else. I spent time in Hastings in a caravan, on the cliff top. If I stood on tiptoe in the doorway, I could see the sea.

The postcards are self-portraits. I'm quite small in some, almost blending in. In others you have to really look to see me. Sometimes I'm obvious, looking out of the scene toward the boundary.

The 1066 Battle of Hastings didn't take place at Hastings. It took place down the road, round the corner and out of the picture; the last stand of King Harold and the 'true' Anglo-Saxons.

English language students stand out with their matching coats, not quite tourists.

Stories of invasion, repulsions. It's a holiday place. No serious walking here. It's fish and chips and a stroll.

In this postcard I'm on the cliff top looking out to sea.

There are a sizeable number of day-trippers. A strange exchange of looks goes on – decisions about who's alien, who's local, who's not. You'll take back trinkets when you go home, memorabilia of the day. These trophies are made in Italy or China, somewhere else.

I kept thinking of Margaret Thatcher's talk of Britain being 'swamped by alien creatures' and Enoch Powell's Rivers of Blood speech. The idea of rivers and flowing waters, the flow that folds back upon itself. The colonised returning to colonise the colonisers. The tide goes out, the tide comes in. It is echoed in the tourist literature about 1066, the 'last successful invasion of England.'

Part of my job is to make the apparent obvious; to see those who appear not to belong; to cross the borders and leave a mark.

It's almost a fiction; the borders are constantly moving. History and the seashore shift, Battle moves inland. The border is right here, or is it 200 yards further on? You've just crossed the border but you didn't notice it was there.

Look at me in this postcard. I'm looking to see what part of Africa I came from.

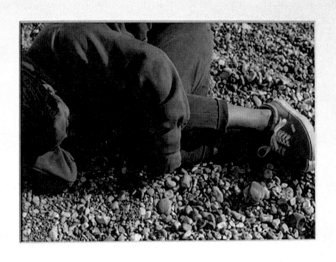

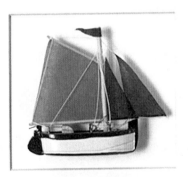

The name of Hastings is of course linked with the last successful invasion of Britain

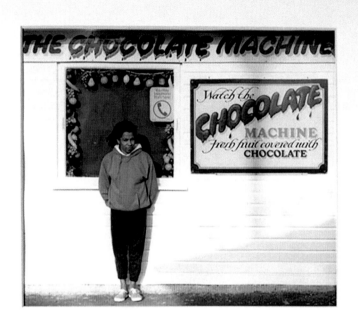

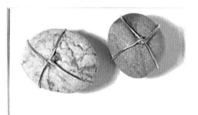

"… and what part of Africa do you come from?" inquired the walker…

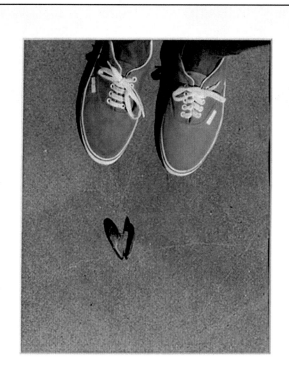

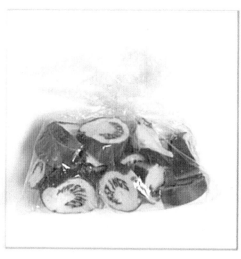

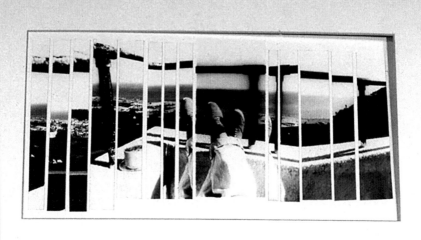

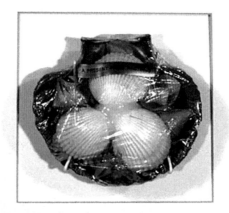

See England under my rule

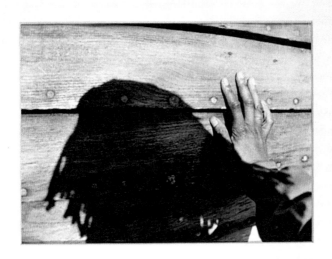

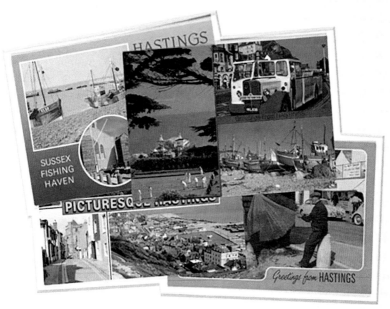

1066 a date remembered throughout the world as marking the final invasion of Britain

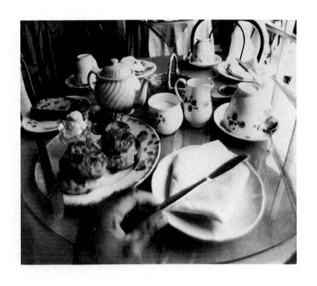

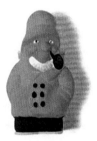

BRIGHTON & HOVE

Georgina Aboud
GROW

My clockless days become ringed with a date.
A Thursday
In April.
Coated in a light jacket and heavy nerves,
I meet a group of strangers:

Grey hands,
Breath is taken in through scarves,
Our boots, laced too tight
are still mud-free.

My mother always said small talk is not for the gifted.
When our voices finally shake loose,
None of them talk small.
Why try?
We are in the airs of ancients and legends,
Where the Devil can finally be thwarted.

And now overlooked by travelled skies,
Ears are sharpened on breezes,
Touch on bark,
On deep pile moss that should replace roads.

A spring cracks open whilst we are on these hills,
Hatching lambs, calves,
Salvaged orchids.

All witnesses to generosity,
To a change in stature,
On a green soaked land.
We grow a community,
You and I,
In chatter and in silence.
We grew a community.
Planted in earth, in food, in April, in May.
In full bloom, by June.

Georgina Parke
THE DOVES OF MOULSECOOMB

A murder of crows descended. First, they ate my harvests,
calculating greedy eyes as hard as their beaks. As I tried to
scare them away, defend my fruits, their attacks increased and
their numbers grew. Desperate gestures to move them just
exposed those tender vulnerable parts to the emboldened.

Turning on me, they pecked me to the bone, and then
my bones clean. Qualifications hard earned, ceased to have
value or be in demand. My beauty, now ravaged by chronic
stress, suffered: colour leeched from my skin and my strength
collapsed.

They pecked at my eyes until they oozed. Lenses
closed over with a thick, dull glaze, rendering all I saw ugly
and broken. I looked around the council estate in
Moulsecoomb, the disemboweled part of Brighton I had to
move to, and saw little but a vortex of destitution. I lost my
way and vision for myself somewhere amidst the labyrinth of
crooked brown terrace houses, scarring the landscape with

their tangle of neglected gardens, besieged by weeds and rubbish and beat up cars.

Last, they pecked at my heart, and grief and loss poisoned my joy and love, leaving me bitter and self-reviling.

Yes, a murder of crows did this, and they didn't care.

I was drawn to a chalk path lacing up a hill behind my house: a bone path really, I recalled from my A-level geology, left over from a tropical prehistoric warm sea teeming with life. Having been raised out of those primordial waters, how sad to be so disconnected from that familiarity now, drained and parched to a crumbling landmass. A path of bones. I was just bone. Bone upon bone.

I walked daily, finding my way in a kind of resonance and affinity, finding solace in the companionship of a path of flint, bones and broken dreams to walk off my grief. The winter easterlies tormented me, accelerating over the hill as a lone gnarled blackthorn leaned trailing in the wind. Somehow I girded myself and my bones grew stronger and denser. I was not knocked from my bone trail.

As winter rains fell, the path limed, becoming treacherous to walk on, but I moved with precision and focus and did not slip or fall. Soon my heart began to well with courage, balming those grief-pierced wounds. As the winter peaked and iced, those 'bitterlies' sliced into my glazed eyes, tearing tears with their icy nails. Slowly a bit of the glaze started to dissolve, and I could see clearly what lay around my feet.

Over the hill and into a wild Spring, I noticed the small beauties amongst the fescue turf in my downcast gaze. The strong whispering of the breeze through mixed Tor and Brome grasses to which the Common Blues and Gatekeepers danced. Vetch, flowers delicate yet bold, in vibrant colours: imperial purples, desert ochres and exotic shapes, grew in the spaces between grasses where sheep's teeth do not reach.

I felt the warmth of the sun as it arced over the hill, smelled the blackthorn blossom. Sometimes I smelt salt from the sea. I heard the birds, I saw traces of other visitors: fox, rabbits, a stoat dashed shyly past.

I grew curious about my companions and started to call them by their names. Some I remembered from school obsessions, others from gardening shows, and those I couldn't look up or find, I made up new names for: secret names that only a heart could understand. Finally, I named my closest friend, the hill, *Lor Chu - Strong Bone Hill*.

I felt the support from my friend everywhere. No longer did it bother me to walk the one mile uphill from the No. 25 bus stop, because this path was held by *Lor Chu*. I no longer cursed my garden, where roses resisted rooting into *Lor Chu*'s bony side - I understood. I took care to walk lightly and be thankful that on *Lor Chu*'s side I had a home.

Spring strengthened as the sun crested *Lor Chu*. I hummed to the insects, called back in mimicry to the birds, and sang sonorous lullabies to the calves as they rooted and licked the fence posts and scratched their heads on the barbed wire. I felt known and seen again; the familiarity and friendship with *Lor Chu* meant that I was no longer a visitor or trespasser but an accepted and welcome sister. There was an ease in the difficulties of the terrain, a yielding and quietening.

Determined to see if I could find a horizon broader than my hope and self respect, my heart lifted my eyes, sweeping past the rusting plough and over the top of hedgerows of hip haws and elder. Resting, and all facing upwards, upon *Lor Chu's* furthest side, which descended to Bevendean Down, was a large beye of white birds. The air was still and blue and the sun Easter yellow. A tranquillity throbbed in the still blue air and even the grasses were still. I paused at this marvel. There are doves in Moulsecoomb! My heart surged with wonderment and hope. I felt something magical had revealed itself from the mundane. Not wishing to disturb them with my bold gaze, I headed in a different direction.

I continued with my daily walks but I did not see the doves again that week in the showery weather. Their memory was etched on my heart, and every time I thought on the sight, I smiled warmly within. A week later, under similar conditions, I saw them again. My heart leapt - oh to have even such a heart and long lost stirrings of joy. It looked so incredible. I didn't realise how white doves were. I slipped off my shoes and edged along *Lor Chu* for a closer view. As I approached the beye, their gleaming brilliance vanished. A crow turned, winking almost, feathers so black and sleek and glossy they had intensely reflected the light - of the sun or maybe of my heart.

I stood motionless, thoughts suspended in bewilderment. I had felt genuinely the peace and joy of their presence, been lifted with hope. Were they emissaries of light that only a glad and open heart could see as they truly were? Maybe I had never seen them so clearly before. My eyes, dazzled by material trinkets and glitter, my heart brimming with conceit, and my bones strained by the weight of consumerism/consumption, meant I could not see them as anything but harbingers of death and pestilence, hanging around parks and roadsides, scavenging and pecking out eyes and hearts.

As I made my way back home across the brow of the hill, the crows turned back to doves as my perspective softened and expanded: I glimpsed my bare arm. It was a pearlescent sheen, far from the nigger brown and caramel latte and other mixed race labels that I had been known by. As I looked at myself, a radiance shone.

Perhaps if we humans were labelled by our radiance and capacity to reflect the light of our hearts, not of our geopolitical or social oppressions, the world would be better. Perhaps the blackest of skins is really the most brilliant of white. Now I felt no affinity to race or colour, just a resonance to this light and all that was like it. Shining brighter than even *Lor Chu*'s bone path, I realised that I was no longer bone.

Bebb Burchell
A SNAP ENCOUNTER

Spring 1967.

The sun is shining on the new university nestling in the Sussex Downs.

I'm walking with my boyfriend, a fellow student, tall, young, handsome, white. We're holding hands.

We cross the freshly mown lawns, laid out between the red-brick moated award-winning buildings. We climb slowly, and somewhat reluctantly, on this fine day up the flight of steps leading to the library. Essays to write!

Coming towards us, down the steps, another young student couple; they too, hand-in-hand. He, tall, young, handsome, white.

She, like me, young, attractive, black.

As they near us, he catches my boyfriend's eye.

'Snap' he says, and smiles smugly.

Sonny Singh
QISMAT

The waves crashed ferociously onto the pebbled Brighton beach as I contemplated my fate on this dark, cold and rainy night. I stood there. Alone. Music was blasting out of the bars. I imagined myself amongst the revellers, living in the moment, getting drunk and dancing badly to Kylie with no care in the world. Would it be bravery or cowardly to walk into the sea and surrender myself to the water? All these thoughts and voices in my head telling me what to do, what to say, what to wear, how to behave, how to live and how to die.

Suddenly, I realised I was wet and cold, the freezing water soaked through to my trainers and jeans. I stepped back, turned around and walked away from the water. An elderly lady stared at me from the pavement and reminded me of my beloved grandmother. I loved her dearly and imagined if she was alive today, she would say: '*I didn't leave India and Africa to come to England for my grandson to drown in the waters of Brighton beach.*'

As I walked towards the elderly lady, she gave me a warming smile and asked if I was ok. I said I was fine as I walked past and made my way up the stairs. I stopped and looked up at the steel letters fixed to the promenade wall: 'I have great desire. My desire is great'. I contemplated my own desires, and all I could feel was sadness and emptiness.

Marriage was not my desire. Mum often said, 'Couples are matched in the stars, and settled on Earth.' I often asked her why most Bollywood films always told the same story, culminating in marriage, as if that led to transcendence. What happens after the wedding? What about happiness? Sharing? Caring? About physical and emotional love? No one ever spoke of these desires.

Two days later, this Sikh groom is staring back at me in the mirror. My turban, blood red, my beard trimmed to perfection, my *sherwani* outfit sparkled with gold embroidery, and I could feel my wedding scarf suffocating me as it circled my neck. Is this my happily ever after? To me it felt like the end, not the beginning of a new journey. Within hours I would be married at Crawley Gurdwara, the Sikh temple.

Coaches will be making their way down the M23, with Bhangra beats blasting out. Aunties dressed to the nines in bright *sarees* and Punjabi suits with matching (and mismatching) jewellery, clapping and singing along to traditional marriage songs, whilst the men at the back of the coach would be bragging to each other about their latest Mercedes or BMW.

I turned around and faced my Dad.

'*Qismat*', he said. Destiny. One cannot escape from what is written in the stars. I loved my dad dearly, he wasn't a typical Indian father in many ways, and the fact that we had been bought up in Winchester meant that we hadn't had many of the traditional cultural influences, unlike my cousins who lived in Southall, the Punjab of the UK. So how did my *Qismat*, my destiny, lead me to this point?

The person in the mirror wasn't me; this was a predetermined life meant for another. I don't know how I ended up at 22-years-old, a soon-to-be husband, following the same path as many before me. It wasn't forced, but it wasn't my will either. I said I wasn't ready, that I wanted to understand the world and find my own partner in life.

My father tied a headdress *sehra* made of beads and flowers across my turban. I'd insisted on wearing one concealing my face from the world, so no one would see my tears. I had met her twice in the last six months. A pretty, softly spoken 20-year-old girl with silky black hair and brown eyes. I wondered if she felt the same. I should have told her, been brave, honest. I imagine her now, immaculately adorned, like an Indian Maharani, her hands and feet painted in *mehndi*, her red Punjabi dress glittering with gold and her face embellished with expensive jewellery. I can almost hear the chime of her bridal anklets as she walks down the aisle towards me. Maybe to her they are like chains tying her to a traditional married Sikh life.

I had grown up feeling so alone. I often heard Mum and Dad talking about me. 'He's just sensitive. They can't all be the same,' Mum said. I did gain some temporary escape when I moved to Brighton to study Economics at Sussex University. I loved Brighton – full of diversity, where anything goes. I often jogged or walked for miles along the beach, trying to forget all these perplexing thoughts going around in my head.

One hot day, walking from the Marina towards the Palace Pier, I focused on a man in white shorts with hairy masculine legs walking in front of me. As he stopped and bent down to tie his shoelace, he glanced in my direction and gave me a smile. He was handsome, with short dark brown hair, dark green eyes, perfectly matching his jade green shirt with a few buttons undone exposing his hairy chest. I carried on walking behind him, focusing on his strong masculine legs moving one in front of the other as droplets of sweat ran down his calves. We both stopped at the pedestrian crossing by the Pier.

'Hi, there mister, are you following me?' he said, with a cheeky smile and a heavy French accent.

Nervously I replied, 'No not at all. I'm off to the Old Steine bus stop.'

'I'm Pierre.' He held his hand out.

I shook it. 'Rajeev.' The touch of his palm, the brush of his hairy arm against mine, created a feeling of sexual desire within me.

Pierre had lived in Brighton for four years and was in his final months of his PhD. We walked together to the Old Steine, talking, and got on the number 25 bus to the campus. As the bus was busy, I sat next to him. My thigh brushed up against his; our eyes interlocked. I had such a desire to kiss him and for our bodies to be joined together.

Pierre and I quickly became lovers. I was inexperienced, nervous, and had no idea what I was doing, but with time, I learnt to adapt to the matching rhythm of our bodies. It was a summer romance, mostly physical and passionate with no talk of the future. A few months later Pierre left and went home to Paris.

Am I destined to be just another Indian man in the closet? I thought as I sat in my brother's Audi TT, as we drove to my life sentence. He made chit chat as I looked down at the gold border on my *sherwani*. I followed the floral design of the intricate embroidery and noticed some loose threads. That is going to be my life. A thread soon to be permanently stitched into a predetermined life.

I could hear planes coming into land at Gatwick airport. I wasn't paying attention to what my brother Akaash was saying. I didn't care. The car came to a stop. My heart started to beat faster, my eyes welling up, I don't know how I am going to get through this day, and the rest of my life.

Any minute now I would see the bright orange colours of the Sikh temple and hear the Punjabi Dhol drum playing loudly to announce the arrival of the groom. I slowly lifted my hand to move the strands of my *sehra* that covered my face.

'Akaash, what the hell are we doing here? What's going on?'

My brother turned to me, removed my *sehra* and spoke. 'Rajeev, there is no *Qismat* in life. You need to find your own way, follow your own path. Quick, get out, you don't have long.'

He went to the boot, pulled out a bag and thrust it toward me. From his suit jacket he took out my passport, some cash and a boarding pass he had printed off. I was shocked, overwhelmed. I hugged Akaash and more tears started to fall. In that moment nothing else matters but to go, to escape. The consequences of our actions and the heartbreak I was leaving behind didn't matter right then. I took off my turban and scarf and left them in the car and watched Akaash drive off. Then I turned and ran.

As the plane took off from Gatwick airport, I looked out of the window and saw the bright orange flag over Crawley

Gurdwara. I saw crowds of people, colours of *sarees* and suits so bright they created a Pride rainbow effect. Tears streamed down my face as I imagined the chaos on the ground: my Dad screaming at Akaash; a thousand aunties surrounding my mother, consoling her but secretly enjoying the gossip.

It was for *her* that I felt the most remorse. I felt ashamed at the blame and shame she would have to endure because of my selfishness, because I was the man who had jilted his bride at the altar.

Five years later, I got a call in the middle of the night. Akaash was sobbing and couldn't speak, so he passed the phone to his wife. Mum had suffered a cardiac arrest and had died almost instantly. I froze, my stomach in knots.

The last time my mum had seen me was my wedding day. She wasn't the most loving of mothers, but she tried in her own way, and I gave her allowances for the tough childhood she had endured. The eldest of eight children, an alcoholic father, poor housing conditions and no education, which was the norm back in Punjab in those days. Getting married to my Dad at 17 was probably the best liberation she could have hoped for.

I landed at Gatwick and took a taxi directly to the temple. I could feel my heart beating faster as we approached. Five years earlier, these same people would have been here expecting to witness my wedding. The hearse had arrived and some of the men were carrying Mum's coffin into the temple, with Akaash and Dad at the front. I waited for everyone to go in, before I took off my shoes, covered my head and walked in.

I made my way through the mourners who were crowding round the coffin, all attempting to say their final goodbyes and finally reached my silent mum. Dressed in a cream Punjabi suit, with a lace veil covering her head, she looked peaceful and beautiful. I placed a rose on her chest and gently kissed her forehead. 'I'm sorry mum,' I whispered.

I felt an arm wrap round my waist and turned to see my tearful brother, his wife by his side carrying their new baby. We hugged, cried and stayed together for the rest of the day. A few cousins and distant relatives greeted me and gave their condolences, whilst most of the aunts and uncles blanked me.

Later that day, I overheard some aunties talking about a cousin who had recently divorced and another who had married a Muslim. 'No shame,' I heard, 'the poor parents.' As I walked past, they made eye contact and stopped me. One aunty hugged me and said how pleased my mum would have been that I came. Another one butted in, 'No point coming when she's dead.' Although harsh and blunt, there was so much truth in that statement. I politely said goodbye and left them to their idle gossip. I'd booked a flight back the same day so I wouldn't have to stay.

As Akaash, his wife and I walked out of the temple, there was Dad, crowded by mourners as they started to leave. I had avoided this moment all day. I felt sick. With a thousand stares on me, I spoke. 'Hello Papaji.'

He said nothing but turned and gave me a soft hug. He put his right hand on my forehead - the mark of a blessing - and looked attentively at me as our eyes met for the first time in years. Then he released me, said goodbye, and turned to speak to other relatives.

On the way to the airport, Akaash told me Dad was persisting in travelling to Sultanpur in India to perform the last rights but Akaash refused to dishonour Mum's final wishes. She told Akaash she wanted to be scattered at Seven Sisters, which made me tearful as I remembered the many times, she would take Akaash and me there. She loved to walk along the river as it opened to the sea and then stroll up towards Beachy Head. He asked me to come back for the scattering ceremony and I said I would try, but I knew I wouldn't.

At the passenger drop off at Gatwick Airport we hugged and said our goodbyes, and the last thing Akaash said to me was: 'Rajeev, come home soon.'

I cried as I walked away, running away again, like I had done years before.

Years passed and my life became a routine, work taking me from one country to another. I developed no meaningful relationships and the internal turmoil of guilt and loneliness never diminished. I felt so lost, with no place to call home and no inner peace of mind.

Rubi, a recently divorced Punjabi girl from Leeds, was the only true friend I had. She had moved abroad for a new life to free herself from a sexless and loveless marriage. One drunken night we had a heart to heart, and I finally poured out my secret. 'I'm never going to marry a woman.'

'I know,' Rubi replied. We both laughed and that night felt like the beginning of the rest of my life. Rubi downed the next shot and said, 'Rajeev, you can't change the past as it's already happened. You can't predict the future, so why worry about something that hasn't occurred yet? All we can do is focus on the present.'

Rubi was right, I couldn't change the past, but I could learn from it, and sculpt out my own path in life. Like a switch my life changed. I left work and travelled around New Zealand and Asia and started seeing the world in a whole new light. I slowly let go of the past, of my guilt and anguish and started to accept myself. *Qismat* is not predetermined. It's just a word that people use to accept one's current way of life.

Six months later I returned home and rented a flat in west Brighton – well, Hove, actually. Akaash and his wife helped me settle in, and I quickly built a life, joining various clubs and getting back in touch with university friends. Brighton seemed so different: there was a new shopping mall at Churchill Square, the shops in the Lanes had changed, and mum's favourite Coop store on the London Road had been turned into student accommodation. I thought to myself, all things evolve but the soul of a place remains.

A year later, walking through the Pavilion Gardens, I came across people dressed in World War I costumes and heard lots of Punjabi and Hindi phrases. I discovered it was an event called 'Dr Blighty', remembering the Indian soldiers who fought in the First World War, and how the Pavilion became a temporary hospital for the injured Indians. It made me feel so proud to be an Indian.

Tears ran down my cheeks as I remembered my grandmother and mum. I always thought granny had an imaginative and creative mind, making elaborate stories up for attention. 'Your grandfather fought for this country when he was young and years later, we had to leave India in the middle of the night to escape death and torture during Partition.' She told stories of women jumping into wells, houses being burnt, of bloodshed and gunfire. I realised that the freedom and life I had was partly due to the life choices made by my ancestors, and if not for them, I would probably be a closeted gay man farming in the fields of Punjab.

As I walked around the gardens drinking my latte, I exchanged glances and smiled at an attractive man sitting on a bench reading his book. As I sat down next to him, I was mesmerised by his dark brown eyes, his wavy dark brown hair sweeping over his forehead, and his trimmed beard framed his face to perfection. A few minutes later he looked over and smiled. 'Hi, I'm Danyal,' reaching out his hand to shake mine. The touch of his hand was electric, and his smile led me towards his warm inviting eyes. He was half Israeli, half English and was visiting Brighton for the weekend.

We talked all afternoon and in the evening stayed for the Dr Blighty projection show. It was magical: the Pavilion was lit up with vast images, sweeping across the building, accompanied by powerful orchestral music. Squashed amongst a thousand people, Danyal held my hand the entire time as we laughed, talked, drank and learnt of each other's lives.

Two years later and here I am again, looking in the mirror at the Sikh groom looking back at me. My *sherwani* outfit has a simple gold leaf design matching my scarf, which is loosely draped around my neck. I turn towards Dad; he straightens my turban and places an exquisite gold brooch pin into it.

'That's better, now you're ready to get married.' He gives me a big hug and says, 'Rajeev, it's time to live.'

Danyal and I got married at Brighton Pavilion, a few hours later. A year later as the sun shines down, I walk along

Brighton beach with my husband and look up at the now rusted steel letters, 'I have great desire, my desire is great'. It gives me a great sense of pride that I didn't give up on my desires. I feel like someone. Me.

Jenny Arach
BRIGHTON BEACH

In my mind's eye I see what you saw
Our fathers in shirt and tie
Trouser legs rolled up to the knee
Afloat in a boat upon the sea
While you and your sister with bobbed hair
Played with pebbles along the shore

Our fathers brought together by the
Kosher meat they preferred to eat
An African and a Jewish man
A butcher and an engineer
Sailing between the piers

The grand old West Pier where my mother used to dance
And the Palace Pier where my brother's took a chance
Playing truant on the rides and amusements

English summers of yesterday
Of seaside trips and friendships
That became lifelong, grown in waters
Of liquid mirrors and silver shimmers fallen from the sun.

Sheila Auguste
GOOD GIRL

The train snakes slowly around the bend into Brighton station, and comes to a shuddering halt at the platform. I should be on the train with Dad, not waiting on the concourse.

When we were children, he would take us on day trips to here and there: it wasn't the destination that was important, it was the train ride. We liked to go to the end of the line. We'd travelled on British Rail trains with tables; the large windows made it feel as though I was sitting in the landscape on a magic carpet, just like in my library book, *Tales of the Arabian Nights*.

Dad works for British Rail. He's based at Temple Mills in Leyton, East London. I don't remember a time when he didn't work there, although I know there have been other jobs. When Mum and Dad muse about the old days, the first few years when they were in this country in the 60s, they laughed about the disgusting jobs they had to do.

'Your father would come home covered in white dust from head to toe when he worked in Dix Asbestos, all in his hair, everywhere, dragging it through the house. And when I worked in that cake factory, I would be standing in six inches of water… or was that the Tate and Lyle place?'

All the way from St. Lucia to the night shift in a factory. It was years before anybody knew how lethal that white dust could be.

When I was a child, Dad's British Rail uniform looked very serious to me. Heavy duty dark navy material, and a peaked cap with the silver British Rail insignia stuck in the middle, like a brooch in the wrong place. My little brother and

I were always playing with this cap; he could never find it when it was time for him to leave for work. I liked to wear his jacket, I enjoyed the weight of it, huge and heavy, with the scent of stale Old Holborn rolling tobacco and his spicy Bay Rum cologne. It made Mum laugh, me clomping around the house in the jacket and his heavy-duty steel-capped work boots.

He's off the train and on the platform. Brighton is the end of the line. His steps are deliberate, hands deep in his pockets. He takes each step as though conducting an experiment to see if he still remembers how to walk. His feet turn outwards and he looks like a slowed down Charlie Chaplin, his trousers baggy at the ankles because he never tightens his belt to the correct notch. A slender, nutmeg-brown man, hair greying at his temples.

He glares at the ground, talking to himself, stands still collecting his thoughts, his face tilted up to the curved girders of the station roof as though they are floating around up there. There are a few starlings swirling in the rafters, jibbering and jabbering their usual nonsense. He rubs his chin, the other hand on his hip; as usual, a grimy off-white handkerchief fell to the ground when he pulled his hand from his pocket. He bends from the waist, stoops to pick it up, causing congestion and confusion around him.

At the ticket barrier, with no hesitation, he looks straight at me. 'Good Girl,' he says and smiles with his perfect white false teeth. They disgusted me when I was little. He'd leave them in a glass in the bathroom overnight, soaking in a sterilised glass of water, like a horrible experiment in a laboratory, teeth that grew on their own in a test tube.

I complained to Mum. 'Why does Daddy have to take his teeth out? Why can't he leave them in, like everybody else? He looks funny when they're not in.'

She told me that one day he went to the dentist with a toothache and came home with no teeth. His gums bled for hours. The bucket of water they used to soak the cloth he was using to staunch the flow turned a deep ruby red, and the water looked like a bucket of blood she said.

I'd invited them both to visit, but as usual Mum was wary.

'Brighton? That's not in London is it?'

'No Mum, it's about 60 miles away.'

'60! Oh, that's far.'

I find it difficult to believe that she left the Caribbean and travelled to England with three children: my older sister and two of her sisters' children. Two weeks on a boat. Where did she think she was going? Not far.

Before we leave the station, Dad turns and points at the few small birds circling the vaulted glass and iron roof.

'They're not seagulls,' he says.

'No, they're starlings, Dad.'

I'm going to take him home on the bus and show him the sights along the way: where I do my shopping, where I work, the Palace Pier, the Pavilion Palace. I'm going to take him to my home and make him a strong cup of PG tips with lots of sugar, and a bacon sandwich – special purchases bought just for him. I'm going to show him around my little house then take him onto the Brighton Pier.

About an hour before sunset, I start bustling him out of the house. We are going for a walk on the pier to watch the sunset, I tell him. Not into the jangling discordant sounds of the arcade with slot machines and crashing coins, but to promenade in the fresh sea air on the side that faces the setting sun, looking towards the ravaged but beautiful outline of the burnt out West Pier.

I'm hoping to introduce him to the greatest show on earth, hosted and performed by my soulmates, the starlings. I say nothing – I am anxious. Will there be a murmuration, a sound that starts small like maybe a gigantic bee on a hot summer day, and becomes a cacophonous celebration underneath the length of the pier but especially beneath the fairground? Or will they just bed down for the night, flying low, skimming the water for their last feed of the day before roosting in loud harmony under the pier?

I say nothing for fear of disappointing him, but I stare nervously and intently up at the sky, and then I catch my breath with the childish glee that happens every time, no matter how many times I am blessed with the spectacle that is about to happen.

'Look Dad, our friends from the station.'

He watches as a small flock joins with another and then another. His mouth falls open. 'What are they doing?'

What has started as a thin fluttering black trail across a blue sky, becomes a dense black cloud, then a diaphanous net of hundreds and hundreds and hundreds of starlings staking their claim to Brighton.

Migratory birds, immigrants like my Dad, like me too. Just before sundown they perform this mad synchronised dance across the sky, never touching each other, swirling around each other, avoiding each other, with the backdrop of a different type of sunset every time. We stand at the railing as they swoop and swirl above, whilst more of them head in from above and behind the buildings strung across the sea front. The flock moves sinuously, flowing this way and turning as one mass. They makes shapes in the sky, hundreds and hundreds of them forming into one giant great whale, shimmering above us in the wrong place, sky not sea.

I cannot explain how mesmerised I am by the murmuration. It is an out of body experience, standing at the seafront, inhaling salty vapours from the water, with dusk approaching rapidly and the red disc sinking fast into the horizon. They turn and turn, and spin and spin and I am spinning too, in this direction and that, and suddenly I am flying with them all in a mad adrenalin rush under the pier searching for my roost for the night. These migratory birds with no borders to worry about, no fears of Brexit happening to them.

They look as though they are being tossed and thrown by the wind, but their wings are flapping, frantically, frenetically, as they change direction with the wind and each other. They are sharply defined triangles in dark silhouette against a patch of sky that is peachy pink, tinged with the bluey grey of dusk, and finally, as one, they turn and swoop beneath the pier leaving a few fluttering starlings that become invisible with the final setting of the sun.

'Time to go Dad.'

I've never been to a pub with him before; he will have a whisky or a Guinness. It is in a perfect location, with a sea view, and I will say to him, 'Not as nice as the beach in St. Lucia, eh Dad? Too many stones. There's sand under the water though.' And he'll reply, 'No, no, but you've done all right, not too bad, not too bad at all.' And then at last I will launch straight in, no preliminaries. 'So, what were you like as a kid, Dad, and why'd you come to England, and how come...?'

He's not really coming to Brighton to visit my new home. I was still a 21-year-old part-time resident of the crumbling house in Stratford when he died. I'd see him around the house on my way to here and there. Never time to stop and chat; nothing much to say to each other. But I knew he was enjoying my life, his daughter the university student. That had always been his plan.

Why did he leave St. Lucia? Common sense, and the stories of thousands of others, tell us that he was an economic migrant. Nothing going on for him over there, so a handsome 30-year-old man with rotting teeth, packs his bags and catches a plane, or boards a ship – I don't know which, and Mum doesn't know, or can't remember. But maybe it wasn't that - maybe he had a broken heart, maybe he was on the run from the police or a woman, or perhaps he came to get an education. Like the one that he ensured I got.

He wasn't really an intrusive father. He left all that to Mum. He only intervened if it was something to do with education or 'qualifications' as he called it: 'Your *qualifications* are the most important thing.' After I failed to get the grades I needed for university, I took to my bed for two weeks. I'd let him down. I knew he couldn't love me anymore. He came to my room, sat on the bed dressed for work, told me it would be all right, that things don't come easy in this life, you must fight for what you want.

Our last significant conversation was about six months before he died, when I conveyed to him in a strangled whisper that I would be leaving my business studies course in Birmingham to study Social Sciences back in London. I don't remember his reaction; all I recall is that I shook with fear when I told him. It felt to me at 20 that this was the first time I had behaved contrary to his expectations.

Six months later he was dead in hospital; the asbestos dust killed him. *Mesothelioma*, it said in tiny writing on the death certificate. He didn't live to see me become the first member of our family to achieve a higher education. I never got to impress him, impress him with my intelligence. I always had the idea he thought I was a hard worker but not that bright. I am my father's daughter after all, and it matters to me that he died thinking I wasn't all that clever; that degree could have proved I was smart and 'good'.

My dad taught me to do the two things I love most: to read and to write. He made me a member of the library when I was four. He carried me on his shoulders to my first day of school because it was snowing and left me in the charge of one of the mums whilst he went to buy me Lincoln biscuits because I was hungry. He spoon-fed me until I was six, because, just like him, I was a fussy eater.

Dad called me 'Good Girl' in a rhythmic melodic St. Lucian accent, but always wanted me to speak 'good' English with no hint of a cockney accent.

I was 37 and he'd been dead for 16 years when I moved to Brighton. Haynes Alexander Auguste was my dad's name. He was known to everyone as Hazel. I always planned to call my daughter Hazel.

I have no daughter, no Dad. It's the end of the line.

Josephine Hall
THERE ARE MORE SHELLS HERE

With Brighton out of sight
and out of mind. My thoughts wander
to Cornish cliffs and Scottish shores.

The shells remind me of these other homes,
other prisons that I felt the loss of so acutely.
Homes that were brittle and heavy to carry
and yet that somehow held me completely.

Home is a mystery to me.
Some days I have many
and some days I am lost;
no shore to run my tears down.

As a child, I would point to the sky
when they asked me where I came from,
why did I look different to them?
Today I still look to the sky for answers.

I find them, I lose them, I absorb, I renew.
This existence is a matter of survival.
The sea, the sky, the shells – they know this
and they do not fear it.

Sometimes when I'm watching the sunset
I want to climb inside it.
I want to live and breathe that beauty.
So why don't I?

I know I must have night so I can have day,
yet when my own sunset happens... I hide.
I dress shame up in different ways
and it multiplies.

Sea air brings a rhythmic reflection,
the tide wears down my defences
and I am no longer ashamed.

Now, like the shells, I am exposed
and enduring.

Zaid S Sethi
CONRAD

'What are you reading?' A girl, blonde, speaking with the confidence of innocence.

'Conrad,' I said.

'He was a racist!'

'A Polish racist?' I asked.

'Maybe.'

I thought of the many reasons why she might have spoken to me. I discounted boredom because the journey wasn't long enough: 22 minutes to Victoria. The others were born of vanity.

We'd just left Purley, the noisiest of suburban stations. I got on the train in a stupor: the transcendent state commuters achieve to get through countless journeys of a lifetime, leaving tree-lined streets of comfort for the bustle of crowded pavements overflowing with desperation. I wasn't particularly annoyed at the interruption. Any irritation she might have noticed was the result of surprise. Despite English spoken without a discernible accent, I knew her to be foreign. Mimicking an accent is easier than the construction of sentences in a foreign language. I have nothing against foreigners, since I am a displaced grandson of Empire.

'I studied him in school.'

'Really,' I said, 'this book in particular?'

'Yes, *The Heart of Darkness*.'

'And did you read him as a racist writer?'

'We were told he was racist. How did you know I'm Polish?'

'I didn't. I was referring to Conrad.'

'Really?'

'Hmm, sort of. Sorry. I guessed you were. I didn't mean anything by it.'

'It's okay. I won't call you racist.'

'Thanks,' I said, smiling at her generosity.

'And anyway, not many people guess my nationality. Well, at least not as easily as it is to guess yours.'

'Now that may be considered racist,' I said.

'Yes, I suppose so. Sorry. I didn't mean anything by it,' she said aping my apology.

'No, of course not. But you mean 'ethnic origin' not 'nationality', I said, correcting her, 'because I'm as British as you are, unless you're still Polish.'

'I was born here.'

'So was I.'

'Good, then we're two British foreigners.'

We laughed.

That was basically how we met: me, 27-years-old, on my way to work, and an arranged marriage inevitably in store for me, and she, 21-years-old, on her way to uni to finish her degree in useless studies. Our journey was too short to learn much more than that she, after the excitement of two years in halls, had decided to return to the predictable comfort of home for her last year. Living at home was, she said, worth it, in spite of the interfering watchful eyes of doting parents. I guess living alone wasn't much fun.

At Victoria station we said our good-byes with ominous threats of bumping into each other again. As I walked out of the station, I smiled at the absurdity of chance encounters.

It must have been a couple of weeks before we happened to meet again. I was looking out for her in a manner of speaking.

I was sitting in *my* window seat (because all window seats are *mine)* and moved without looking up to allow an inconsiderate passenger to squeeze into the middle seat beside me. I was mildly irritated because the middle seat usually remained empty until we got to East Croydon, the station where commuter belt refugees converge for the final part of their journey.

I had long finished Conrad. Despite the racist label attached to the author, I failed to notice the colonialist stain in the story, found nothing offensive. That my white brethren looked down on those with my ethnic hue was only natural. The colour of my skin was not mine to notice. If I was white, I'd do the same. And, anyway, 'otherness' has its benefits. Despite the work of eminent post-colonial sociologists, the natives still endow me with oriental exoticism; my discerning culinary diet, an incomprehensible language, and quaint beliefs. For my part, I viewed my Polish friends in much the same way; stodgy food, Slavic incomprehensibility, and their far too mystical Catholicism for my Church of England school upbringing.

'So what are you reading now?'

I ignored the question as something asked by one stranger of another, not intended for me. My silence was met with an elbow jab. I turned, with an apology rising in my throat. The apology coincided with recognition.

'Sorry, oh, hello.'

'Can't believe you were ignoring me!'

'I wasn't. I didn't see you.'

'Well, it seemed like it.'

'Elbowing me is a strange way to get my attention.'

'I thought you deserved it.'

'It's okay,' I said. 'It didn't hurt.'

'There's still time. So?' she said, looking at the book I was reading.

'Faulkner.'

'Ah, I see you prefer imagined communities.'

'Not entirely imagined,' I corrected her. 'Anyway, I don't think places matter. Everywhere is like everywhere else as far as human experience is concerned.'

'Only an immigrant would say that.'

'You seem to suffer from your immigrant past!'

'At least I'm honest about it.'

'What does that mean?'

'I mean, you seem to exaggerate your Britishness by ignoring your ethnicity, while I am happy about being Polish.'

'I thought we agreed last time we met that we were British?'

'I think we agreed 'we were two British foreigners,' she said with a smug smile.

It was pleasant to note she had such a detailed recollection of our first meeting. It was worth a try: I wasn't foolhardy enough to believe a third chance meeting was possible.

'You read a lot!' I said.

'You do too.'

'Isn't it amazing that we both like reading.'

'Made for each other?'

'Maybe.'

'Yeah, sure.'

'Let me send you my phone number,' I said.

'Why?'

'Just in case you want to meet up.'

'And what about you?'

'Of course I do. Why else would I want to give you my number?'

'Give me your number,' she said. 'I'll send you a missed call.'

'Ok,' I said, and did.

'Name?' she asked.

'Let's use Conrad for now.' I laughed.

'Okay, and I'll be Nellie.'

I waited two days, not to come across as too eager and then sent her a message asking whether she had time to meet up. She didn't reply. Two further messages were ignored. I guess we learn from our mistakes. A few days later I got a message from Nellie. It was short. 'Friday, carriage three, Purley, 7.46'.

I wrote back immediately, 'Great!'

When we met on Friday, I was prepared.

'So, what are you reading now?'

'Jerzey Kosinski.'

'Aren't you trying too hard?'

'What?'

'You know, Conrad, now Kosinski?'

I made out as if I didn't know what she was talking about.

'Both Polish writers, dah!'

'Kosinski's American, Conrad English,' I said.

'Like us?'

'Yes,' I said, 'but you're right. I am trying.'

'Yes, you are.'

The awkward silence that followed unnerved me by the time we got to Vauxhall; just one stop from the end of our journey together. Latent adolescent desperation goaded me into action. 'How about meeting up?'

'Why?'

I considered her too intelligent not to read my mind, but explained anyway. 'Because I haven't said half the things I've been meaning to tell you. Are you free tonight?'

'No.'

'Tomorrow then?'

'Maybe.'

'Okay, look, send me a message letting me know when you're next free.'

'Okay.'

Another silence.

'So, you've been rehearsing, have you?'

'Yes.'

'In front of a mirror?'

I laughed. 'Well, yes. But not whole speeches, just snippets, sound bites. Distilled conversation… like Conrad.'

By the time we got to Victoria, the five-minute journey extended by caring signal failures to about 10, Nellie had agreed to meet up later that evening. She had a tutorial and could meet up after it, if I didn't mind waiting.

I didn't mind.

She was an hour late. Her tutor's fault. Like all academics, she lacked the discipline of punctuality. As Nellie had to be home by 11pm there was hardly enough time to have dinner. We caught the same train home, my stop further up the branch line. As the train left Purley station I wondered whether I could have kissed her goodbye. 'Never mind,' I thought, 'Saturday is only a day away.'

The next day I received a message saying something had come up. She didn't say what it was, and I didn't ask. I was disappointed. I sent her a nonchalant message: 'No worries, speak soon.' It wasn't the cleverest of responses. She didn't contact me for a week. I guess learning takes time.

Nellie rang me the following Friday asking me what I was up to that evening. I told her I was meeting up with friends from uni. She said she would be happy to meet my friends. When we met, I was pleasantly surprised to be greeted with a kiss. She still had to be home by 11pm, and I made sure she was. It turned out to be an earlier night than planned, but the 'girlfriend act' didn't leave me much choice; I couldn't let her go home on her own. Nellie was a star when it came to alienating my friends as most girlfriends are. I should have minded, but it was fun seeing them unable to cope with this new friend I'd found. And anyway, new girlfriends always take priority over enduring friendships.

The 11 o'clock curfew she observed each time we met didn't help us consummate the relationship, but sex didn't play as desperate a role as it had done in the past. For Nellie, it seemed to provide more comfort than fulfilment of desire, which I found strange, but didn't explore. Though ecstatic climaxes have their place, what I found with Nellie was equally rewarding. It was as if we'd sated our sexual curiosity in earlier relationships.

It was about four months or so before she agreed we could have a weekend away. Friends joked about how unimaginative I was in taking Nellie for a dirty weekend to the seaside. In my defence, I'd suggested a city break but she didn't want to risk it. Her parents would ask too many questions and, if she lied and something happened on the holiday, they'd find out. Nellie had obviously thought it through a lot more than I had!

I hadn't told my parents about Nellie either. It was one thing to having sex-driven clandestine affairs, but completely another matter to announce I had a white girlfriend who had the potential of becoming a daughter-in-law.

We took the train to Brighton. We hadn't booked anything and walked down to the seafront to find somewhere to stay. The weather was good, no rain, and our backpacks light. We had two wonderful days in our imagined community by the seaside. We walked along the beach holding hands, stayed out late, kissed, hardly slept and, most of all, talked so much that we were hoarse by the time we got back to reality. But, for all that, we never raised the subject of our families, their prejudices, or our inability to confront them. It was as if we knew.

On the way back, the mood was sullen. We sat across from each other, interrupting our view of the landscape with pathetic smiles. I asked her if she was all right. She said she was. I said I was too. We changed at East Croydon. She asked if I'd mind if she didn't wait for the branch line that would take us both home. I said I didn't mind.

Over the next few days I called, but she didn't pick up. I messaged her asking whether she was okay. She was busy with family. After a long silence, three or four days, she said we needed to talk. She suggested coffee at Victoria station. I knew what she wanted to say before she said it, but I let her take her time. I stayed behind when it was time to go. I lied about meeting up with friends in London.

Was it sadness I felt, or relief? For a long-time, I told myself we weren't enough in love for things to have ended differently. Then again, perhaps there are still those, like Nellie and myself, for whom prejudice is a yoke as real as it was for our parents in the age of first generation immigrants.

L Oluwafemi Hughes Jonas
BEYOND BORDERS

It's Monday 16 October 2017. As dawn breaks over Brighton, I'm unprepared for the extraordinary event about to unfold and what for me it would disclose. I only know I feel unsettled by 'something'. Radio 6 babbles on about borders, walls and Brexit. It's 14 months on from the schism of that vote. There's a questioning tone about 'Britishness' and who belongs here: a tone, all the more ominous, as its reminiscent of my experiences in 1960's and 70's. I avoid going too deep.

My head is full of 'must do's'. 'No time waste!' I hassle. But, unfocused, feeling stuck and irritated with myself, I can't settle to anything. My face **is** a stormy tempest as I enter the kitchen for a late breakfast. My long-suffering husband PJ bears the brunt of my brunch-grump.

'Must we listen to Radio 6? Can't you tidy up a bit?' I say with a relentless crusty, munch.

The Boomtown Rats blares out their song, 'I Don't Like Mondays'.

Momentarily, I know I'm feeling low. Something says 'Stop! Reflect on what is going on deep down'. But do I pay much heed? I guess not. I just procrastinate with 'ting and ting'. A day not unlike some days. Except !

Not long after 1.30pm, just as the kettle whistles on me to make tea, the sky slowly darkens. An eerie, muddy, mustard-coloured haze spreads across the skyscape. As PJ and I stand staring out from the inner sanctum of our home, nothing and no one seems to move.

'It must be a thunderstorm about to crack!'

Anticipating a deafening boom, followed by a deluge, we wait and are still waiting as the ominous darkness grows, creeping soundlessly and steadily over our streets, turning our windows black. Even with the house lights turned up bright, we cannot dispel the dimness. Yet, not a drop of rain falls, no dramatic lighting or thunder roars. Just a loud silence. Now, provoked, street lamps glow yellow on the new ochre and tan mood, hovering above.

'It couldn't be a total eclipse. We've just had one deleted,' I speculate.

PJ murmurs something about pollution, climatic responses to our damaging lifestyles. Given this apocalyptic vision, we park our worst fears, shifting our focus to what the ancients would have made of this phenomenon.

'A bad omen', they'd say, worried they'd not prayed sincerely enough, or lived up to the standards of the Sun God.

'Just imagine,' PJ says. 'The Egyptian Pharaohs and people standing hushed, looking up, transfixed with fear.'

'And the dread,' I add, 'of an immobilised moon, stuck, as if forever, over the sun, blotting out light as a punishment for their drunken misdeeds.'

We laugh, our tension eased by the Pharaohs' imagined fears.

3.30pm. With more stillness, my mind turns again to 'musts': must write that resignation letter. I've already followed a strong urge to let go of other things that were hugely important to my life for a number of years. And yet simultaneously my stomach tightens in anxiety about a loss of purpose, loss of status and relationships: people with whom I've done community projects and who'd become friends. Who will I be now? What am I worth?

It was a muted question I'd asked myself on leaving a hidden world in a Scottish Christian orphanage after 10 years. The institution snuffed the very life and spirit out of thousands of girls, who were meant to have received care. Aged 14, I was re-entering a world unknown, with no history and no map of an 'I' or me, feeling as brittle as cracked glass.

Yet, I am lucky to be alive, to have a father and a home in which I can live. Kathy just five years older than I, my unofficial guardian in the institution, a delegitimised child, had nothing and no one waiting for her. After several years, producing three daughters and grandchildren, Kathy gave up on life. I ponder now on how good people lose sight of their ideals: the survival of flawed systems becoming paramount over thriving children.

Clocking-in at the clothing factories at aged 15, I, an 'only' Black woman in nylon head scarf and overall and headscarf, joined in the laugh and crack. Disguising my padded armour, covering up an unsteady gait, as if fending off an unspoken shame.

'That Darky,' and worse, I overheard. 'We should stick to our own kind,' they said. Then it had no name: the ghost that relentlessly defamed. The 15-year-old I, stuffed it away in a shed somewhere in her head. But that time she heard her best friend refer to her in those terms, she wanted to shed her skin, scrape it off till it bled. Years passed trying to counteract the critics, those crazy crickets in their high-pitch whining. 'You're not…' 'You can't' 'You're too... die-dee die, die…' 'Something in you is a crime,' a whine, whine, grind. I went on stitching Levi jeans in the factories in that internalised carousel. Stitch, stitch, stitching for 15 years and became as faded as those old blue jeans. So jaded was I, by the daily drudge and humdrum of the sewing machine, I barely noticed something growing in me. I'd weaved into the fabric something bulging at the seams: my secretly whispered hopes and dreams.

Until one day opportunity called: 'Hey You!'

'Who Me?' I said, with a raised brow and wide eye. I dived into an unknown abyss. Anything had to be better than this. Now, for a third time, I entered another foreign world, still brittle as glass, among the mainly white middle-class at Sussex University, and the scary workplace of the 'professional' class.

These places where there's no room for feelings. No space for experiences to be met. No room in the house for the unspoken white lines between us. The frontiers borne by any one seen as 'not us'. To those a muted voice says, 'Something with you is wrong.' 'Fit to my norm.' 'Do not storm.' 'What? I, this woman of African and Indian heritage, from a mining town in Scotland? The one who is sunk and depressed by something unaddressed, some part unexpressed, dispossessed. It started in the institution, something I could not name or claim. Except later, when I heard Nina Simone sing 'I Got Life', she expressed an abiding pain. Demanding respect and social justice for those too lost or well, too damn compliant. It took many years, but eventually I laid claim to Nina's 'Mississippi Goddamn' kiss my ass' defiance.

It's 5pm. The sky is a more mellow yellow. Letting go of even trying to let go, my tears fall as I allow myself drift, to find out what needs to be met in the darkness. 'Aaaah,' a voice says so tender and velvet. 'Rest up now, my dear sister, I've sent those crickets packing!'

6.30pm. Having tea. Radio 4 announces that Hurricane Irvine has blown Saharan sand over England. It was said that even Portugal's now raging wild fires belched out plumes, drifting, mingling dust, soot and sand over our shores. Pictures come in of extraordinary tangerine skies, aflame across the country.

'The Egyptians might have been right,' I muse. News quickly moves, linking Brexit Borders and Multicultural Britain.

'Well!' PJ announces, 'No borders could've prevented Saharan dust coming over here. Air, rivers, oceans gonna flow wherever .. blow emissions and all!'

On the multiculturalism debate, one disgruntled interviewee jibes, 'We were never consulted!' My thoughts turn again to the unspoken: the fragility, fear, or aggression, towards the threat of the 'other', 'not from here', the unaddressed, a forever blurred-out mystery. Behind all, may lie our unspoken history.

Again, PJ cuts in: 'No walls can erase identities British Africans, Asians, Caribbeans, Muslims... been here for centuries! It's a crock of bullshit!'
I double up, laughing at the manner of his proclamations.

'When I lived in Scotland,' I say, 'everyone felt awkward about 'the colour thing' Some people meant well you know! Sought to make you feel OK with what made them feel uncomfortable! 'Och' they'd say. 'We're aw Jock Tamsin's bairns' 'Wir aw the same."

It was PJ's turn to laugh at my broadest Scottish accent. 'Yet you heard it so many times, you knew something was stuck in folks throat, never fully spoken.'

'They might have said,' PJ cuts in again. 'We 'are all Kunte Kinte's barnes."

Proving one should never try the Scottish vernacular with an BBC English accent.

Later in bed. I think about the walls I and we put up in ourselves. What happens to our humanity when we wall off our own or others' feelings and experience? Ignore the impacts of social injustice, on all vulnerable creatures and on our earth? When these are only half-addressed?

Tuesday morning. I open my curtains and see hovering over our street a glorious red Indian sun. The mist has not quite lifted as I go out walking, following the mild temperature. I'm enjoying the quietness that still pervades the streets.

Clouds part to reveal a blue window. Crimson and magenta, star- shaped dahlias in a window box flirt. As does the Regency-style roof of one white house framed with lilac peonies climbing a trellis. Workmen have dug a deep pit on part of the pavement; I can smell the earth in the autumn air.

As I turn onto tree-lined Windlesham Avenue, autumn's coat of green, red and amber makes me smile. Leaves float down, silently joining others in a heap along the sidewalk. Wading among them, I enjoy the swish-swashing sound. As I continue on path towards Brunswick Square's green lawn, the silver-blue sea opens into view.

I'm reminded that I live among great beauty every day. Fortunate to have a home and food, to walk on the South Downs, to discover secret gardens and ancient hidden churches that have revealed themselves to me over time. I daydream about the forays I've made since my factory days, into mountainous places: the snow peaks of a Himalayan range, the sense of being a tiny speck in the valleys of the Pecos De Europas, a fern-covered massif in Northern Spain, in the majestic mountains of Snowdonia and the Lake District carrying the sound of waterfalls, foaming, gushing into the river, carving stones round and flat as she rolls. And my favourite grandmother of a fig tree in Cape Tribulation rain forest, in Queensland.

How far I've come from that barren place: the first half of my life, that wore my sense of self thin, that can rear itself, still with its disrespect and internalised oppression. I've learnt not to put up walls to loneliness, to acknowledge the unaddressed, which also belongs to the collective.

Letting go of who I should be, I step into being the writer I am, to tell the story, to make the unspoken speak, to make the invisible visible. I let my hair be kinky and free! It's time to address what really matters: to make no one a migrant or stranger in our hearts, to know we all belong to the land.

Stepping into this new era, I am not alone, for I take 300 black women with me wherever I go. With many colours, I step up to be a guardian of the future, with reverence for our Mother Earth. She cried out in the darkness of that Monday 16 October 2017 for awareness in action to bring hope to future generations. Let us bring the spirit within of this abundant Paradise with no borders, so we all can live.

Georgina Parke
WET HAIR

Soft piles of hair tumbled onto the blue polished floor at Chez Dominique, dampened by my tears as I realised this visit was not the assured trim and tidy up.

Released from my head, the peaceful afro clouds showed little trace of the knots and mattes that had exasperated my white mother. Triumphantly, she patted my few remaining inches of hair into a round ball. The hope of emulating the prettiness of my Peaches n' Cream Barbie was utterly lost. At six-years-old, I did not recognise myself, neither did my form teacher nor my classmates. Strangers would pat and bounce my hair without my permission, like I was some novelty creature.

My family encouraged me to smile in gratitude at people's natural and friendly curiosity. It was surely a sign that they accepted me. It was rural Lincolnshire, however, and I was a curiosity. Growing up in a white step-family as the only black person, there was no one else to share this indignity with. My family were preoccupied with trying to convince me that I was the same as everyone else. Of course, no one else was convinced, and neither was I.

As I entered my tweens, and my hair slowly grew long enough to be fastened into a ponytail, with a Fergie bow above, I whispered a vow of protection of my dignity and identity. No one would ever cut my hair or touch it again. I would never be seen with afro hair nor even doing my hair.

During the occasional family visits from Lincolnshire to Northampton, I would plead for a bottle of Luster's Pink Oil Moisturiser stocked at Joyce's, the black hairdressers. As the bottle got low, I would ration it by adding in careful measure, a squirt of Baby Oil, three tablespoons of warmed Vaseline, half a pot of Brylcream and a splash of mum's Opium perfume. I cautiously dabbed the pink, gloopy mixture into sections of my hair, interrupting the dance towards the light of each individual strand as it worshipped the sun. My hair folded and bowed obediently in a greasy fudge. Such alchemy!

My closest friend during my teens and twenties was Dark and Lovely. Like all relationships, it had its ups and downs. So, it left my scalp oozing with burns for a few weeks… so it sometimes dissolved and broke patches of my hair. It wasn't perfect, but when I would blow dry my hair, I looked indeed, 'dark and lovely'. I had boyfriends, and I certainly felt safer and fitted in better at the large City law firm I worked in. I was one of three intakes from ethnic minorities: one a Sikh, with her long glossy hair coiled like a fat black racer pinned to her head, the other a Jewish male. I believed that keeping my hair French plaited, or straight with a flick at the bottom, was vital to present a trustworthy and intelligent image. I was determined not to let my hair distract or raise suspicion or make any of the partners or anyone else feel uncomfortable. But I was uncomfortable. It took me hours. Also, I had to maintain a high level of vigilance to ensure that it never got wet or damp lest what was styled in hours, was undone in seconds.

My boyfriend booked a surprise wind sailing session one weekend. No amount of cajoling would get me in the water. I had grown up by the North Sea, but there was no pressure to go in, thus there was not the issue about getting my hair wet. Fierce Arctic winds whipped the waves to imposing heights, and the deep clay flats of the sea bed were often so unsettled, that the sea was brown most of the time. Low tides would go out for miles and then curl around quickly when the tide turned. The Skegness Standard would reveal how another unsuspecting dog or its owner had been rescued from waist deep clay. Even the occasional bloated body of a seal or whale would haunt the wide beaches. It was not just 'bracing', as the town motto said; it was a treacherous cold sea and shoreline.

Nevertheless, I missed living near the sea whilst working in London. A chance work trip to Brighton left me convinced I should live there. Murmurations of starlings swirled around the Old Pier at dusk. Lights from the fairground on the Palace Pier scattered across the night sea. There were firework displays, beach BBQs and eclectic events like Paddle Around the Pier. The jocund waves in the cobalt blue waters were studded with bathers of all ages, boats and paddle boarders. These were warm, sociable waters, and although I didn't feel akin to them, as the Caribbean Sea, I appreciated their welcoming and safe participation in the pleasures of the city.

In my mid-twenties, I purchased a seafront studio, and there I would often sit listening to the waves growling through the pebble shore or watching a delicate apricot sun rise and set in an amber haze over the horizon towards the Isle of Wight.

One late summer evening of watching, I became enchanted by the way the glassy waters were illuminated by moonlight. Replying to some mysterious silent invitation, I left my flat, walked across Marine Parade, down the steps and onto the beach, shrugged off my clothes and waded into the sea to bathe under this numinous light.

A playful wave lapped over my shoulders. Despite the seepage, my bun remained dry. Shortly after, I caught a full face of wave. I wiped the salt from my eyes and untangling the heavy, sodden bun, I lifted my hips allowing the sea to take my weight and tilted my head back. My scalp was soothed by the coolness of the waters, and my head felt so light. Sea fingers combed through my hair, teasing out the knots, playing with the repressed coils and dancing with the kinks. My hair undulated around me like fine, silvery seaweed, illuminated by the soft violet light. Years of struggle and shame loosened and was carried off somewhere through the waves. Only the background din of mirth of the evening's revelries was faintly audible. I floated and dipped carefree beneath the waves, as free as a mermaid for one night.

After that evening, I felt willing to be seen locally with my hair in a natural style despite some apprehension that people would stare or try to pet me, or see me as less than them or different. I drew strength from Brighton being a rare place where people somehow found the courage to be more of themselves. I loved bathing and had many more sublime moonlit swims.

Eventually the waters healed my hair traumas. Releasing myself from my vow, I had several generous haircuts. I ceased straightening my hair, and after regular deep conditioning treatments in London salons, I discovered that after getting wet, my natural hair did not return to a tangle of hissing and fizzing medusa-like snakes but to a bed of soft, springy ringlets.

Hayat Nezameddin Shehab
BEIRUT TO BRIGHTON EXPRESS

So you finally left that see-saw city, your marital quilt, guilt, and all that you had built over the last two slip-sliding decades in Beirut. You went there thinking that a country could belong to you, after years of growing up in England with a too-foreign name and knees that were bruised from too many falls from the ropes that divided you. You thought that, in returning to a distant place you barely remembered, the long-smothered H of your Arabic name would emerge from a forgotten place in the throat like a reborn story.

So you fabricated your own story of return, its pages messily glued together by your mother's yearning for escape and backward-facing dreams; her bags had never unpacked, and her feet had always moved to the tabla-beat clack of a place on another continent that had long been razed by dealers of a drugged war. So when guns were momentarily put down, she stacked up her bags and left a terraced red-brick house that she could never call home. She left seeking an absent, mythical place that she never did find, not even in the cedar-lined villages of her grandparents or the dusty, blind streets of her childhood.

And so, at the age of 27, you boarded a five-hour flight from Heathrow to Beirut, taking only your indignant dog and a badly played saxophone, and swiftly you became a queen of reinvention, losing and finding yourself during 20 years of trying on new skins, but so few of them fit your out-of-place dimensions, and all the journeys in all your unspoken dreams found their way back from the hectic highways of Beirut to the blue-white arches of Brighton station.

Pulled by your own backward-looking schemes, you padded your knees and smiled with inconsolable relief as you said goodbye at Hariri airport last summer, but this time you were not a small child fleeing war and clasping an anxious mother's hand, but a woman running quickly out of decades. You tried to leave behind the shrunken skin that you had wound tightly around yourself, but it boarded the Heathrow-bound plane with you, and what you did leave was the scent of jasmine and a vast Lebanese sky that you had tried to hold up with those hopeful small hands of yours, a sky that still held you closely in a crushing embrace that you no longer wanted.

Will you miss the ground that had carried you on its pock-marked back for the hefty second chapter of your adult years? Will it miss your feet, your weight, your stumbling, searching steps?

And in the frenzied days leading up to your Brighton return, you had carefully packed the tattered back-and-forth suitcases, filling them only with your best new clothes. There was no space for your mother's favourite crystals, the baby albums, the paper and ink, the kitchen sink.

You also left behind places that still hummed with the indelible memories of your two children learning to walk around a low bamboo table, of yet another war expected and averted, and of a family that once was almost whole. You left the stories that still float around those now empty rooms, stories that will be half-remembered, half-invented, of evacuation to Cyprus by the Royal Navy on the HMS Gloucester in the summer of 2006 and of lying to your children (they're thunderstorms, not bombs, my darling). Some of the memories that lie behind you cannot be told; they exist only in roaring cold whispers inside you – of days and nights spent injecting morphine into an IV drip and crouching next to a smiling mother's cancer-beaten body.

So when you packed, you left the things you could no longer carry outside the Sussex-bound suitcases, sealing them tightly with colourful scarves, but not tightly enough, it seems, because, here, in the land of your dreams, the swirling colours of a rose-tinted evening near the arches of the bandstand take you back to the smoggy sunsets of Beirut, the belched diesel, and the unyielding traffic that made you ache for the kinder silences of home.

But as that other home collapses into months that now shuffle into the distance of continents, you've started to collect the yellows, oranges and blues that somehow slid into your travel bags: the perfect curl in the middle of your daughter's three-year-old forehead, the open arms of a grandmother's second-floor apartment on Bliss Street, graciously expanding itself so your son could play football in the gleaming white marble of her living rooms, the freshly cut parsley, mint and lemon blending with the music of seven cousins at serious play, their citrus notes echoing in the abandoned dust of chandeliers.

And now all your suitcases are empty and safely stored under beds while the voices of that other time and place tiptoe around you like timid rose crystals. In the quiet of your sun-lit afternoon, you sit on a too-new blue sofa in a red-brick home off the Old Shoreham Road, finally surrounded by four perfectly still white walls.

Priti Barua
MURMURATION OF STARLINGS

Rippling through the rainbow city with the Pride festivities in full swing, dancing across the strawberry sky, a murmuration of starlings was ignited by a spray of purple foam. On the stony beach, the figure of a lone woman trailing barefoot, deep in thought. The pebbles, sharp and smooth, embedded themselves in the soles of her feet; she winced every now and again remembering.

Suki couldn't get to the bank until lunchtime, so of course she got stuck behind an endless line and two businessmen, whose loud chortles fuelled her impatience. Suki, an English teacher, was known for her methodical and pedantic approach to life, born out of never-ending to do lists.

She felt the blood rush to her cheeks then glanced at the time. Her mobile phone bleeped to indicate low battery. To make matters worse, there was now a 'position closed sign in the window of one of the tellers. Meanwhile, the queue had launched itself out onto the pavement of North Street.

In the corner of the bank, she noticed a smart-suited lady walk to the back where she glared at customers and said in a steel voice, 'You can make cash deposits in the envelopes at the ATM. Just step this way please.'

Suki jumped out of the line and motioning to the lady, said, 'Excuse me, this is urgent. I need to withdraw more than my daily limit at the ATM will allow, and my son is at the Royal Alex awaiting a blood transfusion. Can you help?'

The green-eyed manageress shook her head and in a deadpan voice instructed Suki: 'Go join the queue like everyone else.'

This was the last straw.

She looked in panic at the growing line of customers and infused with fear as her phone finally died, she screamed out: 'Hello everyone, please can you help me? My phone just died, and my son is at the Royal Alex being treated for cancer. I need to withdraw some cash, and I don't have time to wait in this queue... would you mind if I go to the front, please?'

A sea of puzzled expressions stared back at her, and then a miracle happened; the trance was broken and someone took her arm and someone else asked her to breathe deeply – she was hyperventilating – and led her to the counter. It all happened so fast she struggled to catch her breath.

But then the women behind her whispered, 'Oh, that's sweet! As if I believe her.'

'Pull the other one!' another said.

She turned, tears streaming down her flushed cheeks, and nodded in shameful acknowledgement.

'Damned unfair,' James said when she got back to the hospital. 'I'm sorry you had to go through that, Mum. Shall I punch the manageress?'

She smiled at him. 'I just think it's rather poor customer service. Sometimes things happen, and you need a human touch, not a robot.'

'Unforgivable,' James said. 'Karma will find her! Don't worry, Mum. I'm being brave.'

When he was small and had fallen over, he had said the same thing: 'I'm being brave, Mummy!' Who had told him not to cry? Didn't she say it was okay for him to cry - for boys to cry?

Now here they were, just the two of them, on the top floor of the Royal Sussex, high up, looking out over Kemptown's terraced streets.

The sun setting, night stars beginning to burst out, glinting in the blue.The TV screen flickered. No sound escaped their lips. Inner and outer worlds immersed in silence, enclosed in the hospital walls. Imprisoned, confined.

James turned to look up at her. The nasal gastric tube hanging loose out of his left nostril like an umbilical cord. Hanging loose.

Suki smiled at her teenage son. James, 13-years-old, bright brown eyes gleaming, bald head beaming. A is for apple, B is for banana, C is for... the big C. And then everything stopped.

'Mum, it's okay you know, I'm still here. Right now, I'm here!' followed by, 'Can you put 'Final Fantasy' on? I'm going to try and get to the next level.'

And in that moment the most important thing was getting to the next level. James was right, of course. Except this was no Final Fantasy, this was for real. Her heart trembled on uncertain currents as she allowed the sense of horror to absorb her.

This cannot be happening, I will not allow it. And yet it had been allowed. By some unseen force of nature, some strange despotic God she no longer believed in.

'Mum grown-ups are so strange. They're always worrying! Thinking about the future or the past. I'm here now, that's all I know, so I just take it as it comes. Really it's that simple.'

Some things, like black toast, leave a bitter taste. The mouth is soured. Life is not the same as it once was. When you think back, it's not the bluebells and buttercup syrup, it's the blackness of overdone toast you'll recall the most, though James told her once, 'Carbon is good for you. Just look at the stars. We are made from star dust, did you know?'

Did she? Not that she'd care. Feet firmly rooted, in Jesus sandals, nails varnished, sparkling like stars on the tips of her toes; she looked at them in quiet admiration, ignoring his words.

'We are all of us stars, and someday we will know it!' And he would burn brightly as he spoke. Sometimes he burned things on purpose, not like he was an arsonist or anything, not at all, he just ate his bread like carbon. Cinder box fresh.

So now here she is thinking back to what once was. But the blisters are on the inside. Buried deep in the schisms of the heart. And then it dawns on her: It was a very long, long time ago. And yet she finds herself lost in distant memories when motherhood wore her well. Her mind driving through Sussex on that drizzly, cold day. Suki could see the houses and railings and St Peters church as they sped past on the London Road and the reflections in the shop windows, the blur of the busy streets. Raindrops on the car window. All things she saw yet captured nothing on camera. She'd forgotten her glasses.

Ella and James in the back, not wanting to be here now, driving to the travel clinic to have some jabs. 'Jabs, stabs!' she heard James jokingly say.

'Come on guys, we've been putting this off for weeks. Let's get it over with.'

Parked outside, they climbed the stairs to the waiting room and walls adorned with posters dispensing news about tropical diseases like malaria, the killer strain and rabies and Japanese encephalitis, promoting vaccines for all.

Ella stood reading of risks, fear rose but didn't compare to the fear of injections. James looked at her, his brown eyes open wide and raised his brow like the 'Rock'. Ella feigned a smile as she picked at the skin around her fingernails. James volunteered to be first and get it over with.

The minute they walked into the main room, he looked at his mother and asked how long the needle was. His eyes seemed huge now as they glistened with fear; wet tears threatening to fall as the needle was pushed into his arm.

Caressing his face with her fingertips, around his eyes a blotchy rash where he rubbed them to hide the tears, squashing them with his hands before they had a chance to fall. The Doc put the plaster over the jab and offered him a sweet, but James decided he needed the toilet right away. Suki knew he was escaping, anything but this. Even if for a moment.

'Please James if you can hang on for one more? That would be great,' said the nurse, but the toilet beckoned. Dr Sameera suggested he lie on the couch for the next jab.

Suki whispered 'Om Mani Padme Hum' from years of sitting in the meditation hall with the Nepalese monks in the Chiswick Vihara. Maybe her children will be Buddhist converts too? Time would tell. Time was a tell-tale after all. The doctor asked him to stay calm. James became hysterical, shaking his head, and finally Suki had to comfort him, lying him down, like a baby, while she counted to three.

Dr Sameera suggested James come back next week, but he croaked - in weak resolve,

'Aright, okay, we can do it now.' And he buried his face into Suki's body where he was at home, cuddled and safe. She loved him so much. Her little boy, the youngest one, she loved them both.

Then it was Ella's turn to be brave. But the tears soon came, and her big lilac hat was pulled down over her eyes as Suki held her, hugging her tight. James told her to imagine being on a tropical island.

Suki stared at her hands. Brown, medium in size and shape, knobbly knuckles, bitten down nails, a silver ring with an amber stone on her ring finger. She noted it was not of sentimental value in that no one gave it to her. She realised how few material gifts of value she owned. She avoided sentimentality. You never have to worry about losing something if it has no emotional value and so, there were no photographs framed in gilt adorning the walls, nothing to shout of a past or a shared history. None. Ella had long since grown wings and flown, eager to explore the world and all its wonders.

Suki reflected on the party people in the flat opposite, their all-night gatherings pounding out the sounds of wild and eclectic funky tunes. Immersed in a queasiness that had no root, she rose to the bathroom and forced herself to purge. Let it all out. The queasiness would vanish, and she could go back to sleep. But it didn't and she was out of tricks.

It was Pride weekend, and she was thinking about James and their walks on the beach, together. And an impulse hit her to go outside, a gentle stroll to ward off those careless snippets, flashes of the past that were like hungry wolves eating up her insides.

Their flat on the third floor of a newly built block was on Cromwell Road in Hove 'Actually'. As she shut the door, she found herself wondering where she put her passport. She resisted the urge to go back and search for it and convinced her anxious mind that it was in a safe place – probably back in the knickers drawer.

She recalled an ex-boyfriend saying he loved her for this. 'For what?' she asked.

'For your nutty professor ways', he replied. He had noticed the passport. It was in the top drawer of the white plastic crate in the kitchen, in among the potatoes. It had lain there for months, no, probably years after the relationship ended. Perhaps, even after she had become a mother and given birth to Ella and James a decade later.

Well, at least 30 years had passed since then, and now she had upgraded to the knickers drawer. If she was burgled – she doubted a thief would look there anyway – the passport was safe, and she was getting better at holding off on her compulsions.

She turned down the corridor and took 11 strides to the lift. Twelve would be even, so she snuck in one tiny step inches from the elevator door. It hiccupped on its way up, and she was relieved when the door opened, and there was no one inside. Her 12-step rule had led her to bump into strangers at times, but if she couldn't follow through then her compulsions would get the better of her and the panic would set in. Outside the last rays of sunlight began to fade, and she waltzed through the park to the beach.

'If I die mum, will you be able to get compensation?' How can he say such a thing? He cannot embrace death.

'No amount of money will ever replace you!' she tells him.

The doctor has him hospitalised immediately. After all the waiting, she is truly shocked at the speed of the action that follows, and the senior registrar calls her out of the waiting room to explain. Body shaking in convulsive sobs as Suki whispers in an empty hospital room, annexed for quiet shocks like this one, 'I have two children, and I will not let either of them be taken from me!' And her heart is screaming at the faceless God who has allowed this to happen.

She has a foldaway bed beside James in the ward. The days are strange and unexpected. There are other families in the ward; their children suffering from some form of cancer. She can't imagine why any of them have been singled out.

Though deep down, she knows this can happen to anyone. In the daytime, James plays his games, whilst nurses come and go, checking his blood pressure and temperature, passing meds through IV drips into the lines that go into his chest. Cyclophosphamide, vincristine, prednisone, and doxorubicin are the names of all the chemo drugs that are being passed into his body. She thinks the names are melodic, she is angry at an invisible god but praying for a miracle all the same.

In this way the days pass and turn to dusk and the summer sun fades into the evening shadows. One day, James asks her about his life and its reason.

'Everything has a reason,' he explains. Then, seeing her tearful and sad, he asks if, upon his death, he can be sent off in a satellite into space.

She does not want to hear such things, but then he starts speaking of all the stars and his fascination with the universe and he tells her how he wants to go through a black hole, dying like a great adventurer, traversing mysterious boundaries. He has always been this way: curious beyond his years.

'Sometimes I think about God,' he explains one day. 'For all I know, God is inside me, for all you know I am the re-incarnation of Vishnu or Buddha or Jesus Christ.'

Suki continues walking barefoot across the pebbles in quiet absorption, but then she stops, suddenly afraid. For the tears have thundered into her heart, uninvited. An unexpected wave that cannot be surfed. Then a familiar voice inside herself whispers, 'I love you, Mum', and she looks up to see the murmuration of starlings whirling above her head, and in that moment, somehow, she just knows that his ashes are being whisked away, stolen by the seas and the North wind, to be spun in swirls and eddies, wherefore eagles may claim him and spin his carbon ashes all the way up, to sit upon a throne, inside a galaxy of stars. The brightest of bright stars in the Greatest Beyond.

Jenny Arach
AT HOME WITH THE QUEEN

He is African at home in Hove
Where simmering on the stove
Are his supper of kippers
He eats wearing his slippers
Watching the BBC news on TV

Later on in the other room
He plays Gilbert & Sullivan
Old Congolese and Swahili bands
Eyes closed beating time with his hands

Whiskey glass swaying on his knee
A member of the European Economic Community
A toast to the British Queen
Long may she reign

Next morning he is on the quarter to eight for Reigate
Seated with coat and gloves stowed above
Reading the Telegraph and Times arriving on time at nine
Ticket please calls the clerk, everything's going like clockwork

In Dar-es-Salaam he is English on African time

Tuning into the BBC World Service
While eating supper of fish and rice
With beans, greens, peanut sauce and a beer of course

Pilsner glass swaying on knee
Sitting on the balcony
A member of the East African Community
A toast to the Commonwealth Queen
Long may she reign

Next morning along Samora Avenue
He reads the Daily News in the Daladala queues
Watching the bus boys call and hiss at the Swahili Miss
They *kuss kuss* in the hope she will board their bus.

WEST SUSSEX

Sally-Claire Fadelle
TURMERIC FOOTPRINTS

High up on the South Downs, above the village of Hassocks,
in West Sussex, Jack and Jill windmills stand. An idyllic pair,
retiring together in 1907. At Jack's side, the remains of the
earlier Duncton windmill, whose past is little documented and
often overlooked, in much the same way the history of my
people is. Jack still attached to Duncton mill, his ancestral
forefather. All three, Duncton, Jack and Jill, relics of a bygone
Sussex, stand undulating on Clayton Hill, in the heart of the
county. A hill once called, Duncton Hill.

    'Where does bread come from?' I ask the children on
mill visits. Most often the resounding answer is Tesco. I ask

them where does it really come from, the flour to make the bread, where does that come from?

'People ask me where I come from,' I say.

'Sussex, I come from Sussex.'

They ask me where I really come from, my big dark eyes, my straight black hair, where do they come from?

Jack and Duncton mill stand back as Jill welcomes the picnicking public or passing rambler. Today the sun shines bright on the daisy dotted grass. I shiver as the slight breeze catches me. A trickle of people appear at the top of the track, weaving up from the car park. They have come to see Jill mill, who stands resplendent, carefully restored to full working order.

I have just finished putting the information boards outside the mill when, a little girl gains my full attention. Her heavy oiled hair in thick, dark plaits, which frame her shiny golden face. She holds her father's hand, looking shyly at the other children running about as if they know each other. Her mother wears a face of porcelain next to the molasses complexion of her husband. The couple chat to other parents with a slight unease.

My mind drifts back to a little girl, many years ago.

'Your father has been ready one whole hour. I tell you, at this rate we go reach back before we get there.'

The house smelt of masala and jasmine, as my mother combed the oil through my long hair and neatly put plaits in place. My father had begun loading the car with deck chairs, cool box, windbreak and picnic. My brother, mother and I had our final trip to the toilet to appease my father.

A regular Sunday occupation, for us, were these trips out in to the Sussex countryside. The drive was really the best part as, we were contained in a capsule. Mum was keen to get out in the fresh air and to stretch her knees; dad, keen to get there, have our picnic and go home.

It was a steep climb up on to the top of the Downs, the car park disappearing behind us. Huffing and puffing, all four of us spurred on by the promise of a picnic, which meant different things to each. Mum with her encouraging chatter, as she hid any notion of her worsening arthritis. My father listing,

'All de tings I could be doing, if you all ent drag me up here wit all these damn fools, freezing wit a flask of tea. What is this stupidness?'

My brother, younger than me, holding on to our mother in the same way I held my father's hand, tight, tight. Like two stripes, father and daughter, mother and son, trudged up the gritty slope.

At the top, people wandered around Jill Mill and picnicked, stopping briefly, to look at my father.

'Oh, ignore them love,' my mother would say. Mum would send a plea with her sad eyes and hope people would be kind. Very soon they turned their attention back to whatever they were doing, before this dark man appeared, a blot on the landscape of Middle England. My father's faraway eyes tried to smile, a look I would come to recognise in myself years later. He pulled his jacket tight to his chest, as if closing a curtain on this Sunday in early June. His tweed sports jacket, my mother had brought him for days like today, barely keeping him warm, he stood starkly, as purple as the heather and clover backdrop.

I could hear the wind circling us, nearly visible, like fists and fingers, jabbing, pointing, poking. Green rolling hills stretched for miles, unspoilt, but for human nature. Any building fading from view, just a speck as fine as those in the fabric of my father's jacket. I pictured, pink and yellow houses, high up in the hills of San Fernando, far away on the island of Trinidad. My father had no roots in the Sussex earth, the wind could carry him away at will.

The two windmills stood together, clearly defined and defiant against the soft sunny sky. Jack, the tall black tower mill, his sweeps long gone and with them his strength and ability to harness the wind whipping around his brick body. He was now a private mystery and the butt of jokes from children.

'He looks like a dalek,' some would say, 'or a rocket,' others would add.

I would tell them he was a windmill, the same as Jill. They often laughed. Jill the gentle, white post mill, tiny by comparison, with a vulnerability. A more fragile frame of wood. Her sweeps outstretched, set in a kiss, as if shielding Jack from the public gaze; protecting him, as my mother did with my father.

Inside Jill mill, my father explained the workings of a windmill to me. I listened intently – proud of his engineering knowledge. While other fathers were asking the guides, my father knew the workings of the mill, as he did those of my mother.

Mum sat with my brother, waiting for dad and me to emerge from inside Jill mill. Our picnic was not laid out like the other families. Tupperware boxes were opened, only enough, for hands to dip in. Still the smell of curried chicken wings wafted over the Downs. The cheese and tomato sandwiches overcome by this, lay limp and reserved. We all liked Tunnock wafers, and they united us on our picnics.

'You all ready to go home now?' asked my father, visibly blue with cold. He did look smart, if slightly overdressed for visiting dusty windmills at the top of a dirt road. The leather of his shoes had a white layer from the path, as if the ground were trying to bury his footprints, taking this alien out of the pretty Sussex landscape.

My mother began to pack up the few bits she had let out of the picnic bag, which double up as her shopping bag during the week.

'Mummy, why don't we ever use the picnic basket from Trinidad?' I asked, as I always did. I got the same answer; it was full of knitting and she would have to empty the knitting and find a new home for it. It was just easier to use the shopping bag.

'But,' I continued, 'other people have picnic baskets.'

'We are not other people,' came the answer.

The picnic basket was a woven wicker one. It depicted Trinidad in pictures sewn on it and declared, Trinidad, land of the humming bird. It seemed a shame it never left the house, but as I went to say more, my father was quicker with,

'Leave it Sadie, just leave it nuh man!'

'I thought we could have a picnic in Ashdown Forest next weekend,' my mother ventured, in a hurry to change the subject.

Dad did his steups – mum called it his chips, as it sounded like he was saying, chips. We headed back to the car, and so it was most weekends. We worked our way around East and West Sussex, between the strong shoulders of the

Downs. My brother putting ticks in his, I-Spy cars book, mum looking forward to getting there, dad looking forward to getting home and me looking for windmills.

None of us denied that Sussex is a beautiful county, yet we all secretly hated these family outings in its boundaries. It conjured up feelings of being a travelling carnival float, visiting places where some saw us as curious and others just didn't want us there, seeing us a blemish on English soil. My father was the square peg, a black one too. His looks and sing-song voice out of place. My mother an oddity, a self-imposed, outsider and we, my brother and me, like two badly mixed cakes, not made with local produce. We knew, but we didn't understand.

In the hug of the North and South Downs my brother, pale and pasty, not enjoying being out in the sun and a stark contrast to my father, raised questions in strangers faces. Our father, sitting on a striped deck chair in a winter coat, eating cold chicken wings, whose aroma settled on the heather and bracken, dandelions and buttercups, of Ashdown Forest. Me with turmeric tinted fingers, picking daisies on the Burwash lawns of Batemans. Our mother, her hands knotted with arthritis, fighting that pain to endure one greater, on our days out.

Thick sand dunes at Camber meant no feet pebble picking to the sea. My father would run down the sandy slopes and be swallowed up by the waves. The temperature of the water did not seem to hinder him as he raced hard, oblivious only on this beach, to the hostile gazes of the reddened bodies. I would follow him and sit at the edge of the water, staring hard out to the horizon. Trinidad was out across the sea, the pixie boot shaped island. I was fearful my daddy might, one day, swim back home, a home he never really left.

My love affair with the windmills of Sussex began with Jack and Jill. Maybe I could see my parents in them as a child, as I do now. My parents in another life, black and white. I have no markers now my parents have gone, save these windmills. Jack, the tall, dark one on private land, sold from under his foundations as land was taken from my people, the Caribs, the Indians. Jill, still at his side, her sweeps still shielding him, yet now there are families like my family, plural; children like me.

I lead the group in to Jill mill and begin my talk.

'I am going to ask the children this,' I say and after smiles from all the parents, I continue, 'does anybody know where bread comes from?'

High up on the Sussex Downs, inside a white windmill, a little Indian girl says,

'Our bread comes from Taj.'

Jill mill appears to creak, can windmills have arthritis, or was it my mother watching over me? I wait for a quip from on of the other children, or a parent to pull their child away.

'What's Taj?' asks a young lad.

'Kushie, answer the little boy,' says her father.

'It's a shop, like Tesco,' she says avoiding his eyes.

'Oh,' he says.

All the adults smile, and the frost my parents could never thaw up here, all those years ago, starts, to clear. The adults begin to talk to each other, and the children listen to my story of how flour was made.

I go out into the picnic area to see a multicultural Sussex, one I never saw in childhood. I smell curry and naan bread, cheese and pickle and hard-boiled eggs.

Jack and Jill, black and white, they have stood for over a hundred years, together. I glance up from my picnic and see my parents, they belong in the Sussex landscape, as does my brother, as do I, but this is not over.

I head to Jack and Jill as a visitor. I can hear my father telling me the workings of the mill. I see other visitors listening. How sad, my parents did not live to see a day like this, when Sussex was black and white. My father loved the history, of the county, yet we were not a part of it then. Inside Jill mill, I place my hand on the wall of the roundhouse for the final time, tracing her curves, as I say goodbye to Sussex.

Something catches my eye low down on the wall: five small, faint, yellow spots. I remembered as a child reaching for the wall as they began to turn the buck of Jill to face the wind. All the other people were on the other side. I held my father's hand and the wall with my spare hand.

A part of me would always stay in Sussex for there, on the white wall of the mill, my turmeric fingerprints. Maybe one day someone will repaint, but that will only preserve me deep in the wood. Long after I am gone, Jack and Jill, will stand strong as my parents did, all four equally a part of Sussex and Sussex a part of them.

High up on the soft, green carpet that is the Sussex Downs, Jack and Jill are visible for many miles around. I hear them identified – Jill is the white mill; Jack is the black mill. My mother was the white one, my father was the black one. I feel beige amidst the colours of the Sussex landscape, a muddy

126

colour, a colour largely ignored – there are no beige windmills; there are no beige people. I flit like a chameleon through the beautiful county, I can be black; I can be white. The French burr stone; the Derbyshire peak have different lives in a windmill, they lay side by side – separate. Should they meet to grind together, the result would be wasted, impure. It would not be the white ground by the burr or the brown of the peak – it would be beige.

The wild flowers that bloom around Jack and Jill, are the prettiest of colours, shades of yellow, orange, lilac and blue. They mingle; they mix. They intertwine like lovers. I bend to stroke their petals and whisper – make me a beige flower.

Nina Thaddeus
FROM SINDH TO SUSSEX - MY MOTHER'S MEMORIES

I was born Una Sampson on the 16 June 1930 in British India. I was born on what was to become Sussex Day, and it was 22 years later, after the agonising and traumatic events of Partition, which tore my country apart, that I found myself living in beautiful Sussex. The decision to leave my home town and community was agonising, yet I knew in my heart that as an Anglo IndianI had to choose what was best for the future of my two children, and it was with that thought firmly in mind that in 1952, with a heavy heart, I finally left my friends and loving family and sailed away from the newly formed Pakistan.

This was not my first trip to the UK. My father had served in the British Army in India during the Second World War. When India and Pakistan were given independence, he was ordered to report to army headquarters in England. We were part of the last British regiment to leave Indian soil, and I can still hear the pipe-band playing at the Gateway of India in Bombay as part of the stately ceremony as the British Raj came to a close and a new India was born. It was March 1948, and when we docked in Liverpool the army put us on a train to Stewarton in Scotland. My father stayed with us for the first week, but then got orders to report to British Intelligence headquarters for his military debriefing at Maresfield, near Uckfield in Sussex.

That was my introduction to Sussex, a place far away where my father was to live separated from me and my mother for fifteen months. I, at that time had no idea, how importantly Sussex would feature in my life. I was a 19-year-old romantic, and was just waiting for the day that I could return to my home in Karachi and marry the man I had become engaged to four days before sailing to the UK.

The Karachi of my childhood was a beautiful and peaceful seaside town. This view was supported by the US Army, who published a guide book in 1942 for the American military, which refers to Karachi as 'the cleanest city in India, well known for its sea, beaches and bathing, it has the credit of being known as the Paris of the east'.

As an Anglo Indian in British India, I had a happy and privileged upbringing. We had servants and lived in a beautiful colonial bungalow. Socialising, dinner parties and picnics were important aspects of Anglo-Indian life, as were Western fashion, popular music and American movies. However, of most importance was our professional status, Oxbridge education, Christianity and, of course, loyalty to the British, which my family and I had in abundance.

Scotland welcomed us with warmth and curiosity. We ate in the mess daily, and had three full meals, it was all British food, no curry at all. However, my mother quickly discovered that cayenne pepper and turmeric could be bought from the local chemist and she often re-cooked our food with the spice. In June 1949, after a happy stay in Scotland, we were delighted to be sailing back to Karachi, but on arrival we quickly found the effects of Partition had been colossal. We had experienced the anger and desperation of the people leaving and arriving before we left for the UK, and knew that the extreme violence, and volume of people, had created the need for refugee camps and squatter settlements. During our absence our community had diminished as many Anglo Indians had migrated to places like Canada, Australia, and the UK.

The previously orderly city of Karachi had become radically and irreversibly altered, but my young heart remained hopeful, and in August of 1949 I got married. Shortly after, on 26 November 1949, India became a Sovereign Democratic Republic and its first constitution came into effect on 26 January 1950. The constitution listed Anglo Indians as an official minority group in India. While there was no official declaration of minority status for those Anglo Indians remaining in Pakistan, the overall non-Muslim population had reduced to less than 10%.

With the British and the privileged position they bestowed on us gone, the Anglo Indians and those with European heritage felt uneasy and abandoned, and we all began to question further our future prospects. My husband had a good job, we were happy, and my two children were well and looked after, but uncertainty and doubt was everywhere, and we decided to leave.

At the time of immigrating to England the foreign exchange regulations allowed for only £10 per person to be taken out of the country, therefore money was very short. However, my mother packed two massive shipping trunks with huge tins of lentils, rice, ghee, tins of corned beef and lots of dried food. After a very short stay in London, which was heavy with smog and suffering the severe aftermath of the war, we moved to Brighton, East Sussex.

Everything in my life was changing. I was in a new country with a different culture, dialects, landscape and social structure. But I immediately fell in love with this quiet – as it was then – yet grand seaside town. I remember arriving by coach and making my way to my husband's relatives who lived in Regency Square, and looking across the sparking sea, trying to catch a glimpse of the magnificent and exciting Palace Pier in the distance.

On the coach into Pool Valley I had caught sight of the Royal Pavilion with its Indian domes and minarets, which made my heart skip. Just being next to the sea reminded me of Karachi, yet the landscape could not have been more different, with Karachi set in the arid Thar Desert, a complete contrast to the beautifully green rolling hills encompassing Brighton. In Karachi, the beach has black sand and I was expecting Brighton's to be soft and yellow, so was really surprised to see pebbles. Karachi at that time was very cosmopolitan, yet Brighton even then had an international feel about it and because of the tourists and students there was always a sense that something exciting was happening. The whole layout of the town was so different, I had never seen hotels and houses so close to the seafront. In Karachi we had the beautiful Clifton Beach but there were no buildings anywhere near it and the pier was just a long concrete block.

Shortly after moving to Brighton, I had my third child and we were joined at the house by my childhood friend Rosie and her husband, who had also left Karachi. Being faced with having to cook for three children and four adults who still yearned for curry and spicy food was daunting. Money was short and none of us could cook, so it was eggs with everything. We became expert at boiling eggs and served fried eggs to our visitors. Our lunch was often just a bit of bread, which was still rationed. At first, we could only buy what was called the National Loaf, which was made with rice or potato flour with added vitamins. In the evening, we ate rice with a vegetable or pulse dish and occasionally mince.

Only locally grown seasonal vegetables were available at that time so we added whatever seasoning we could get hold of and made bhujia, a mixed vegetable dish. In the winter, it was cabbage, turnips and swede, in the spring and summer lots of cauliflower and green beans. Peas had a very short season and we never saw a *brinjal* (aubergine). We would wait for the spring for the salad and tomato to become available, and after Whitsun the price of salad would come down and we would buy.

I vividly remember shopping at Tesco in the London Road, not far from the vegetable market. It was at that time a pavement stall which sold food in damaged and bent tins very cheaply every Saturday. Turmeric, cayenne pepper and sometimes ginger were only available from the local pharmacist, who included the warm healing ingredients in their blends of tonics and cough medicines. I remembered my mother buying these spices from the pharmacist when we lived in Scotland, and very quickly found a chemist in the Ditchling Road that was willing to sell the precious spices to me, half an ounce at a time.

Interestingly, during the First World War, the Royal Pavilion Estate and other premises in Brighton, became military hospitals for thousands of wounded Indian soldiers.[3] This resulted in *dhal* (lentils) and *ghee* (clarified butter) and a variety of Indian spices being specially imported from India to Brighton in order to feed the soldiers. There was also a special committee made up of Indian officers, who represented the various religions and castes, set up to find and approve the right kind of local English flour to use for making rot's and other Indian breads. (The military links with Sussex and India go back to 1885 when the Royal Sussex Regiment was first stationed in India).

As time passed, we became more inventive with our cooking, and the absent long grain rice was replaced with the more available pudding rice, the much-missed lentils were substituted with dried split green peas. To replace chapatti flour, we made a mix of self-raising flour and wholemeal flour and thereby, with the help of the spices obtained from the chemist, were able to make a more authentic version of dhal, rice and chapatti. I also remember that I could occasionally buy bunches of fresh garlic from the French onion and garlic sellers known as Onion Johnnies, who cycled along the south coast selling their wares door to door, a sight that delighted me.

Brighton's first Indian restaurant, Bahadur Taj Mahal, had opened in 1948 and lasted all the time I lived there, but sadly I could not afford to eat out in those days.

My parents would never have anticipated the life I would have to lead without a cook in the cold climate of England where food was still being rationed, and Asians were still a small community who were commonly looked on with either curious warmth or overt prejudice. Many people said things to me like 'your teeth are so white' or 'don't you speak good English'. I never hid where I came from and generally found people were very nice to me. They were mainly inquisitive, and I always tried to be friendly and never intimidated. I remember being quite shocked when I realised that most people had no idea what an Anglo Indian was, and how little was known about Partition and its devastating consequences.

Everything was a big adjustment and my first winters here were difficult. I found it hard to stay warm and learning to light coal fires, drying washing and only having hot water once a week was a huge challenge.

I also remember the indignation and disbelief my friend felt when she realised that she would have to cook, clean and do her own laundry, and I vividly recall the sense of shame I felt when I first had to clean floors and toilets. As for using an outdoor loo and a 'guzunder' or chamber pot, I was outraged and amused as back in Karachi we had flushing indoor toilettes and outdoor toilettes were associated with servants. These feelings were however quickly replaced by a new understanding of the privileged life that I had taken for granted in India, and a new set of values quickly evolved. I became more than grateful for what I had and what this

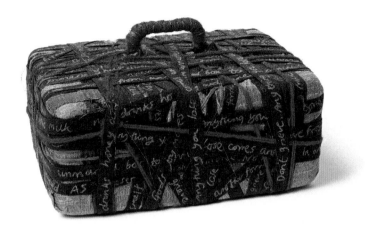

Alinah Azadeh, The Unmarked Box, 2010. Photo: Xavier Young. Collection of the artist.

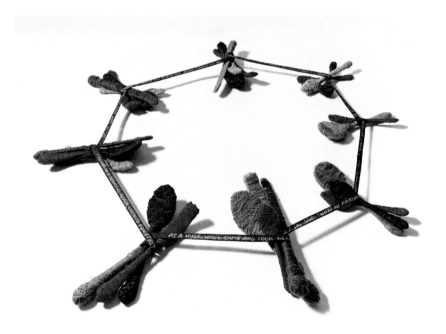

Alinah Azadeh, Gifts of the Departed (II), 2009, Photo: Xavier Young. Collection of the artist.

country offered me and my children. I began to value the experiences and life lessons I was learning by having to start again from the bottom. I also became aware of just how discriminatory society in British India had been.

In 1955, my husband secured a good job 30 miles away in Crawley West Sussex.

Even though thousands were being built, we were not eligible for a council house, so we went to the Commission for the New Towns and got information on re-lets. These were the houses that the original Crawley residents, who did not want to live in a new town or with the new 'cockney' population, had sold to the commission as part of an agreement which allowed them to leave.

The commission were having trouble letting these houses as the rent for a new council house was 7/6d a week and a commission house was £3 a week, which was a lot of money. We got a list of 25 houses to view and when we found the house we loved we signed a seven-year lease. In July 1956, my husband, our now four children and I moved to Crawley.

In 1947, at the time of Indian independence, Crawley had 9,000 inhabitants; when I moved to Crawley in 1956 the population had grown to 29,000. It is now estimated at around 114,767. During the 1950s and 1960s, Crawley underwent massive construction and I have always felt a great sense of belonging as I was there during the time of the town's formation.

Our new home had a fabulously large garden for my children to play in and I couldn't wait to start to try to grow flowers. I remember often stopping in the street and admiring the lovely English front gardens and I loved the way they were ordered, usually with a colourful symmetrical layouts.

In my youth, I had spent a short time boarding at the Convent of Jesus and Mary, in Chelsea, Shimla, which was the summer capital of British India, located in the middle ranges of the Himalayas. I remember the green landscape, rolling hills and cottages with English gardens full of roses, dahlias, geraniums and beautiful blue and white delphiniums, so it was delightful to see the actual English gardens of everyday life that had so influenced the gardens I knew in India.

For a few years, shopping was my main reason for going out. Each Crawley neighbourhood had its own shopping parade and, at first, I used it, but as the town centre became developed I started to walk to town with my small children almost daily. In the early 1960s a very small shop opened that sold some spice and imported vegetables. The Oriental Emporium in Crawley High Street started as a 'hole in the wall' operation. I would go to the hatch and excitedly ask what they had, and what was then seen as exotic vegetables – capsicum, okra, fresh chillies, or a whole pineapple – were sometimes available.

In 1969, Crawley's first Indian restaurant, The Taj Mahal, opened and for many years it was the only Indian food outlet in Crawley; today there are over 28 and Indian food is sold in all supermarkets.

On Sundays the older children and I would walk to church, which at that time was the beautiful Franciscan Friary. It had a low quadrangle of cloisters built around a courtyard adjacent to the church of Saint Francis, it was very gothic and peaceful. The Catholic community at that time was very mixed and I made many Polish and Irish friends. Sixty-five years later

I am still active within the church community and the ethnic mix is bigger than ever. At the time of moving to Crawley, there was only a handful of black or Asian families but that started to change in the 1970s and today Crawley has a thriving multicultural population.

At the time of my arrival in the UK, discrimination on the grounds of colour was not illegal, therefore 'colour prejudice' was generally unchallenged. In 1965, the first UK race relation act was brought in to combat the culturally embedded 'colour bar'. This act was slightly strengthened in 1968, however, it was not until 1976 that an act was passed that made discrimination unlawful in employment, education, housing and personal victimisation. This was the same year that the Crawley Campaign against Racism (CCAR) was formed in response to a letter sent to a local newspaper from the son of my closest friend, who was at that time in Hospital being treated by a multiracial medical team. He was responding to the increase in local racist attacks by the growing neo-Nazi movement. This period was the only time that I experienced a real fear of racism. Some of the attacks with fire bombs, vile propaganda and graffiti were sickening, and I recall for a short period of time not leaving my house in the evening. Forty-three years later the CCAR is still active and I remain a prominent founder member and co-president along with my second husband John.

In my experience, the majority of people are kind and tolerant and the council has always actively encouraged hosting and supporting events that bring all communities together. Crawley was the first town in Sussex to hold an annual Mela and International festival, and the CCAR has held a multiracial social event supported by the town's councillors, MP and police every year for the past 43 years.

At the age of 87, looking back over many years, I feel that being actively involved with so many local charities, political and religious groups and community events has been a privilege, and I take pride in being the founder of Crawley's Interfaith Group. The saying 'there is more that unites us than separates us' has been constantly reinforced during my time living in Sussex.

Sussex welcomed me 66 years ago, and while I have wonderful memories of my life in India, the County of Sussex, especially Crawley, is the place my nine children and I have all called home.

SUSSEX AND BEYOND

Jasmine Harris
BLACK JOY

Finding the needle in the hay
Finding your face in my work
Dripping water from hands
Holding air in mouth
Everything and nothing
The song the world sings but doesn't see

Hayat Nezameddin Shehab
UNSPEAKABLE SEAS

It was years ago that it all began,
as many things begin,

with disappointment and knowing
that this was not the life you wanted.
It was then that you inspected the ropes
and frayed the nets that could have saved you.
Years later, in paralysed silence,
we huddled around your wrecked yellow sofa,
weaving morphine
into blackened veins.
An unthinking storm
crowded upon us
while a distant thunder of gargling
rose out of your silence like deflating glass.
Deadened, we watched your sinking face,
the mouth moving soundlessly,
your brown eyes, unblinking and dulled like destiny.
You drowned in slow motion
over many days, but, like all good sailors,
saved us the pain of a backward glance.

Alinah Azadeh
THE UNMARKED BOX
(from In the Skin of a Stranger)

You are wandering through a garden at night. It's dark; not the deepest shade of darkness, more of an inky-blue, dappled in places. Can you feel the temperature? It's warm, slightly balmy. As you move through the space you feel something brush past your face; leaves, a fruit of some kind; apples perhaps, or pomegranates? You realise you are in an orchard. You seem to be alone but you don't know this place or what you are doing here. You wander through the trees, looking for something, but you aren't sure what.

A sense of urgency to reach the outer boundary of the garden, to find a safe border, an edge, overcomes you. You start to run. You see the silhouette of a wall a few metres ahead of you and stop just short of it. Can you see it? There is a very low section here which has eroded. It seems to be an extremely ancient wall. You run your hand along it, and a crumbly powder comes off in your fingers, like hardened mud. You want to jump over it, but then as you go to lean your hand on it to raise your body up and over the top, you realise that you are barefoot, in pyjamas – and that this is a dream. You startle and wake up. You have this dream many times throughout your childhood. You never get over the wall.

****

It is late Spring, 1992, and you are 24. You are sitting on a coach, on a worn blue leather window seat. Ahead of you, 'God is Great' in italic white sticker type is plastered on the front windshield. The coach is full of families and a few male passengers. All of them – except for you – have their window shades pulled down to protect them from the midday heat. This is the bumpiest eight hours you have ever spent, riding north-west from Tehran to Namin, a small village in Ardabil Province, three hours from the city of Tabriz in Iran, with your mother. She is trying to read a newspaper and making vociferous political comments at regular intervals. This is making you slightly anxious; she was almost arrested on your train trip together last week to the north-east for the same behaviour. But you love travelling with her, just the two of you.

Occasionally she breaks her reading to look up, smile and point out at the landscape in between. A landscape she knows so well and which you are just discovering, on this, your first ever trip to Iran with her, to see her birthplace and the setting of her early childhood. You remember the plan to go to Iran aged seven, which never happened, and then was put off until it was too late, *and the Revolution made a visit much too tricky, darling.*

You have been learning Farsi to prepare for this trip, sitting in the Centre Pompidou in Paris where you live now, with headphones and a notebook, taking a self-managed audio-course, then spending weekends in the Champollion cinema in the 6th arrondissement, run by an Iranian, who sometimes screens week-long programmes of Iranian films. You sit there in the dark, with your notebook, writing out fragments, trying to keep up. It's subtitled in French and you can only just about process the double translation. You feel inexplicably comforted when you see the rural landscapes of the north in the first crop of films you watch, including *Where is the Friend's Home?* by Abbas Kiarostami. Soon you will be there, inside that world, part of which you have some kind of ancestral claim to. Finally. It's a thrilling prospect, laced with trepidation.

You are jolted back into the present as the coach takes such a sharp turn, that you almost knock your mother onto the central aisle. You both laugh out loud; it may be uncomfortable, but it's a real adventure together, the most significant one so far. There are so many hairpin bends on these mountain roads, which, alarmingly, don't seem to have any white lines on them at the edges. And then at other times, far mountain ranges come effortlessly into view, rooted in fields of parched yellow below. One of them catches your eye; a rectangular field in the centre of a hillside, only the rectangle is black, burnt to the edges, with a crest shape in the middle. Your mother explains that this was the crescent of the Shah, etched into the landscape and then set fire to during the 1979 Revolution. Somehow it never grew back, never replenished itself.

Approaching the village, you see it's much greener than you imagined. A young boy runs along the pavement waving at the coach, crying out in excitement. He catches your eye. You smile. Despite the exhausting journey you are excited too, to meet a whole section of your family; an uncle, aunt and cousins you only saw in photos as a child, and to visit your grandparent's grave, grandparents you never got to meet before they died.

The coach stops just opposite your uncle's house, here they call it a villa, a single-storey bungalow with large windows, set on a wide terrace. Your mother taps on the cream, ornamental, slightly rusty metal gates. To the right, on the wall, is a hand-painted message, one foot high, in white and green bubble lettering: *Be khooneyeh Hooshang, khosho- madid* – Welcome to the house of Hooshang. Your uncle, aunt and cousins rush out beaming and all talking at once to greet you both. Light summer chadors, smiles and kisses.

Here they are; your uncle, short, tanned, white haired and bright-eyed, smiling, arms open. His wife, Bahar, a lot taller, dressed in a blue, flowery summer chador, smiling but a little more reserved. Their daughter Mina, with whom you have exchanged a few letters since you were around eight-years-old, offers a smile of recognition and welcomes you in English. They take your cases, kiss and hug you, comment with bemusement on your massive, black Fila trainers and invite you to eat, sweeping you both into the house immediately.

Lunch is *ashe-reshte*, a delicious bean, herb and noodle soup with salty flatbread, pitted with dark brown, crusted dips where stones have imprinted themselves into the dough on baking. After lunch, where you are trying to keep up with what is being said in Farsi but not managing very well, everyone takes a nap. You really need to sleep too, but it's not yet a habit for you, unlike everyone else here. You are too excited to rest and after a while you feel drawn to head outside to the garden.

As you walk down the light sandstone terraced steps at the back of the villa, you realise this garden is an orchard; apple, walnut and cherry trees all grow here. You find yourself wandering through it slowly at first, then feel compelled to speed up, searching out the edge of the garden. You get a strong sense of déjà-vu. Towards the far end there is a stream, running clear and shallow. Beyond it, you see a wall, crumbling and low, at one end. You stop, stand and stare at it, hard. It is as if you are old friends and you want to have a conversation with it. There it is. The wall of your dreams. There is a strong sense of having arrived. In your body and in this place.

You get closer and try to peer over the wall. There is a garden similar in size to this one, with just a few trees dotted around, the ground almost completely overgrown with weeds in between and all around them. It is empty, and feels neglected. You are tempted to climb over the wall and explore further.

As you are contemplating this, your cousin Mina arrives. She has a broad, open face tapering to a tiny, perfectly round chin, huge hazel eyes, and a cheeky smile. Dressed in a light, black overcoat, her long brown hair is loose and uncovered, in this, a private space. She shoots a look at you by the wall and playfully but firmly advises against climbing over it, as apparently the house next door is state property, definitely off limits.

As you both sit down on the grass by the stream, she moves closer and tries to tell you a story about this wall, made of baked mud and hay, that you seem so transfixed by. She is giggling in between sentences as this is the first time she is trying to communicate in English with you beyond a simple welcome. You smile. Even though this is your first day together as cousins, you feel like you know her, from her letters and the black and white photos sent of their family your mother would get from Hooshang.

From what you understand – through the broken English and Farsi mixed up – buried underneath the wall, there was once a box. A heavy, silver and brown metal box, more like a small chest really.

As she starts to describe it, you realise that you know this box! It is Russian. It is covered in decorative filigree patterns and imprinted with the date 1909 on the inside of the lid, and two Cyrillic letters in bronze on the outside. Your mother had it in her wardrobe while you were growing up and gave it to you when you left home. You remember her giving it you in a very ceremonious way, for safekeeping. It has the air of a bona-fide heirloom. You felt honoured. Now you keep special postcards, photos and letters in it, in your studio.

Using her broken English and various hand gestures, Mina tells you the box once contained hundreds of gold coins, made from the forced sale of your family's land back to the state during the rule of Reza Shah. Your mother has talked a lot about him; he was a commander backed by the British and Russians, who supplanted the increasingly corrupt Qajar dynasty during the Persian coup d'état in 1921. Out of this a brand new royal line was created – the Pahlavi Dynasty – who were later toppled during the 1979 Revolution, when Reza Shah's son was in power.

Your mother's family were khans, landowners of much of this area, including some of the border towns with Russia during the previous Qajar period. During that era, these lands were pretty much run in a renegade fashion. The official 'ruler' was your paternal great-grandmother, Ghamar Khanoom, an apparently ruthless matriarch who commanded 200 border guards and, according to your mother, at some point traded one of her daughters in marriage for the port of Astara.

Fearing she would lose the fortune acquired from the sale of this land during the period of nationalisation, Ghamar apparently buried the box underneath the wall for safekeeping from her husband, who had a serious gambling habit. This is a familiar story; you have heard about him before from your mother. Ghamar finally banished him to Russia as punishment for gambling away the entire contents of this box, thus losing a large portion of the family gold wealth, on one fateful trip over the Russian border to Baku at night. Once he left, he was never seen again. So, you reflect, you may have other relatives in Russia – his descendants – whom you will never know.

Your aunt offers a different version of this story years later which is that your great-grandfather left because he simply could not bear to stay married to Ghamar. Apparently this alpha female was so dominating and difficult to live with, that even her own children shook in their shoes in her presence. In the end, she died of poisoning; no one ever found out who was responsible but it is rumoured to have been a servant in her immediate circle.

A decade later, in 2002, your mother tells you yet another layer of the story about the wall; of a great uncle who was extremely wealthy, but also very tight-fisted, and did not trust banks – or indeed anyone. It was known in the village that he hoarded a huge amount of gold which he used to hide inside clay barrels and bury beneath this same wall, none of which have ever been found.

This thread of the story has apparently been around for about a century in local folklore; people still believe the gold is buried there, though the children never found anything. All efforts to find it since have been very minimal, due to the laws stating that any gold found in the ground in Iran belongs to the State, not to the person who digs it up. Striking gold in such a small village – 10,000 inhabitants at the most – would be hard to conceal. You also know that your grandfather, an army general with a love of free speech, women and wine, inherited his father's gambling habit, and that any remaining wealth was lost in the next generation as a result.

Once all the gold in the family had been drained or squandered in one way or another, the box remained empty in the family house. Your grandfather passed it to your mother, who brought it with her to the UK. You remember it in her bedroom wardrobe at home whilst growing up. It was an enigmatic object of great aesthetic contrast to the white formica doors and shelves which enclosed it – the relic of a time traveller. You found this box impossible to open. You once tried when your mother was out but couldn't work it out at all. You had to wait until the time she first opened it for you, the day she gave it to you as a gift.

Here she is, taking your hand in hers, with a gleeful smile, placing it over the secret lock, on the right-hand side towards the back, almost indetectable. It's a tiny silver indent, which she carefully pokes a biro into, giggling. You hear a dull ping as it releases the lock. You peer inside to find stacks of light blue airmail letters covered in blue biro, scrawled in Farsi, and black and white family photos. As you grew older, you longed to be able to read those letters, to know more about who she had been before this life with you, here. After she died, you searched for them amongst her belongings, but found nothing, assuming it went into the hands of your sister and aunt, to those who could read and actually understand what she had written.

****

It is Autumn, 2010. I am sitting alone in my studio in Sussex, looking through old photos, postcards and a few letters in the Russian box, planted on a thick denim tablecloth on my studio bench. I have an increasing desire to wrap this box up in fabric – as I have been doing over the last few months with so many objects left to me by my mother – in a creative act of simultaneous remembrance and separation. But also, in a rather ritualistic way maybe, to protect it – or me? – from all the inherited stories of loss and dispute it carries. Whether obscured, or even lost-in translation, I see traces of them in my own life. But the box feels too big, useful, and full of potential to mummify in this way. It doesn't belong to a dead person, it was given to me to keep safe and use. But still this need to wrap the box arises.

I go out to the kitchen to reflect and make tea, thinking about a recent discovery I made at a show at the British Museum, *Power and Taboo*, that in certain African tribes they wrap the belongings of their recently deceased to prevent them from affecting the living in a negative way. They become totems, ritual objects of power.

On the way back to my space, I notice a metal safe box in the hallway, among a pile of unwanted items marked for the tip. It is smaller than the Russian box, but almost as heavy. It will work as a 'proxy' object to wrap up. I take it back to my table and instinctively start to bind it, using orange and blue silk ripped sari ribbon, and bright red kilim wool from my trip all those years ago to Iran.

I think about the dream, the garden, my late mother lost suddenly in the sea and all the love and care I was shown in Namin. I pick up my book of Rumi poems from the table and randomly open it at a page to find an ode, 'Unmarked

Boxes', which I read several times, taking it in as a clear instruction. The instruction is this; not to grieve, because all that is lost will return one day in a different form.

I write this out, over and over again, in silver pen, on long strips of thick, black cotton. I layer it over with phrases from the rest of the poem, where he talks about how children, once weaned on their mother's milk, now drink a mix of wine and honey.

He speaks of divine love moving and flowing indiscriminately from one unmarked box to another. I layer the cotton strips of texts over each other, binding them around the box, until it's completely covered, like a crazed, three-dimensional drawing, the edges of one line intersecting with another like secret friends.

As I hold the box tightly on the table top, cradled under my left arm, tying the last knot of bright red wool to keep everything in place with my fingers, I feel for a moment like I have arrived on the other side of something – an invisible wall perhaps – am safe, and that nothing has been lost.

Alinah Azadeh
THE FISH
(from In the Skin of a Stranger)

It is late September, 2004. I am sitting at an octagonal, walnut dining table in my mother's flat on the outskirts of a spa town in the south east of England. Ancient trees spread their tapering branches – a spectrum of yellow gold to a blackened brown – across the window vista, reaching out towards a lake at the bottom of a hill at the far end. A secret lake that very few people seem to know about, apart from the residents and some of the boys I used to know, who would creep in through the woods to fish there at night. As an 11-year-old, I used to be able to see the very top of this house from the kitchen window of the mock-Georgian family house I grew up in as a teenager, hovering just behind and above a billowing fir hedge that marked the garden boundary.

Back then this dark gray, foreboding house was said to be haunted; it was occupied by an elderly widower whose children had all grown up and left home. My mother used to gaze up at the house and tell me that one day she intended to live in this woman's house, when she had passed on. It would need some doing up of course! I remember being perplexed by this comment and thinking my father would never agree to that. And then a little excited for her that she might get her independence back once we had all left home. Home was not a happy place to be at that time. Many years later, after her divorce from my father and the death of her third husband, Robert, she went knocking at the door of this house, now under new ownership, painted bright cream and surrounded by an immaculately landscaped garden. She discovered it had been turned into flats and that the ground floor flat was about to go on sale. She put in an offer immediately and finally established her own independent household for the first time since arriving in the UK from Iran, 35 years earlier.

This front room, which doubles up as a dining space where she has regularly hosted parties of 70 people, is full of colour and intriguing detail. On the far wall hangs a half-finished, psychedelic painting by my brother Steven, a collage I made of Iranian women dancing around a fire – and a watercolour in blues and golds painted by one of my uncles in Iran, of a mosque in Mashad, his hometown. An enormous red sofa facing the window from the far wall doubles up as a bed when I come to stay. I sweep my eyes across the photos of family in quirky, elaborate silver frames, the dusted pink chaise-longue, the Iranian and English ornaments mixed together on nested glass tables in corners – and a huge, gilded mirror above a dark brown marbled fireplace. It all brings me a sense of deep comfort; many of these belongings have migrated from my childhood home or from the last house my mother lived in with Robert, like silent friends. The cherished relics of her previous lives and loves.

My mother loves it here; she says it's her favourite home so far, apart from her flat in the northern district of Tehran near the mountains, which she bought quite recently from the rest of her inheritance following Robert's death. She lives alone, but Ralph, her English boyfriend, is here much of the time. She wears his ring but doesn't want to be officially married. *Three husbands was enough, darling, believe me!* This is possibly the most uncomplicated and baggage-free relationship I have ever seen my mother in; mutual adoration, joy – and a new kind of freedom for her. An intense contrast to the 22 years she was married to my father. *He knows how to cry, he is so kind and he adores me really. And I don't even have to marry him!* During the spring, he brings her a basket of fresh produce every week, grown in his back garden. Today I note basil, spinach and tomatoes – all in the salad on offer, nestled inside a large, thick, cut glass bowl. He isn't here today but he is definitely present.

The table is also laid out with a selection of steaming Iranian dishes; lime, kidney beans and saffron scents mingle and permeate the air. A generous side of baked salmon sprinkled with dill sits in a large red, oval dish, ready to be sliced. The table itself, draped in thick, cream crochet, rests on a blue and cream silk Chinese rug below, busy with flower motifs moving in all directions. A muted golden autumn light is streaming in through the three gleaming curved bay windows behind us and spotlighting the steam rising from the open dishes.

My younger brother Steven to my left, head cocked to one side, is retying his ponytail as he chats animatedly to my elder Iranian siblings, Farhad and Firoozeh on my right, about the origins of the English language. The children from my mother's first marriage, whom she left behind when she migrated to the UK, they are both now living here, after a long and somewhat complicated process of transition from Iran. I look at Farhad, noticing the distinctive streak of white running through his thick, short hair from just above his left eye to his crown. Later in life, I notice the same white streak growing in exactly the same position on my own head. Farhad is now studying to be an interpreter, he is warm, intense, full of plans and insecurities. He clearly adores my mother. Firoozeh, petite like me, with red wavy hair and an uplifting smile, has just got married and is studying English and training to be a beautician. Steven is back in town after travelling for four years and trying to do up his flat, a stressful process that *isn't going quite as I hoped*. Something to do with planning. He'd rather talk philosophy and keeps off the subject.

It is lunchtime, and I realise that this is possibly the first time the five of us have ever been alone together here, eating. It is a rare convergence of all those born of our mother, in one space. This recently patch-worked family of siblings is not without its complicated feelings. There is a joviality mixed with an unfamiliar tension that infuses us all being together. My mother is even brighter and breezier than usual, as if compensating for any unease. She treats it as a great achievement, *everyone together now, finally, like family should be, darling.* I smile, struck and moved by her sense of a mission accomplished. Later on this chapter of our lives will feel like a fleeting moment, a blurred snapshot, something fragile and intangible.

Here she is, coming in from the kitchen, wearing a maroon V-neck cashmere jumper, straight jeans and a ruby and diamond necklace given to her by Robert, as a wedding gift. She swoops in with the final dish: *fesenjoon*, chicken baked in walnut and pomegranate – black, thick and sweet. Our favourite. She beams at us all as she lays it down, an almost triumphant look on her face after many hours of cooking from early in the morning. I smell her sweat mingling with her fresh, flowery perfume, Eden, as she bends over next to me. Using sunflower-patterned oven gloves, she uncovers a huge 'cake' of baked rice, revealing a golden brown, perfectly crispy outer skin – *tadeegh*. We all compliment her loudly, 'Bah bah!'; this is everyone's favourite part of the meal. The crispiness of the *tadeegh* is the near equivalent of a cookery medal at every Iranian dinner – and the diplomatic tussling over who gets the biggest slice of it punctuated many of our childhood meals.

As we all start to eat, getting busy slicing through the rice crust and lifting the fish with silver forks and knives especially laid out for this visit, she starts sharing with us all her dream of the previous night. It plays out like this: She is on a beach of white, golden sand, intensely blue water, perfectly clear skies and still, warm air. 'Paradise, really!' She is looking out towards the sea, feeling deeply content, when suddenly, out of nowhere, a huge wave rises up in front of her, 'As tall as this house, darling!' It rolls right up to her, hovers for a moment – then sweeps her away. At this point she raises her eyebrows, bends forward smiling and says, 'Now, children – wouldn't that be an amazing way to go? Come on! In such a beautiful place.... so quick! No getting old and ill, no need for any of you to look after me, you'd be free! No hassle! Simple!' And she laughs, finally serving herself some food.

Since my brother and sister arrived from Iran, she has brought up the subject of who will look after her when she is old a number of times, but none of us take it seriously. She is 68, looks as if she is in her mid-fifties and acts even younger, full of energy and life. Non-stop. A seemingly untiring current of powerful energy. She recently informed me that she intends to live until she is 100 and plans to return to Iran to die at roughly aged 90 – *once I've really had enough!*, employing an Azeri nurse to look after her in her mountain flat in Tehran, *where she will bother no one and you can all get on with enjoying your lives. Just as long as one of you has some grandchildren first, agreed? I'll let you all off caring for me but there is a price, ok?!*

My younger brother raises his eyebrows at the description of the tidal wave and starts talking about Jung and dream symbolism. My sister says 'Wow, Mum, what a dramatic way to go, just like you!' And Farhad agrees, chuckling and shaking his head. And me, I smile too, but settle uneasily on the image of a huge wave for a moment, recalling a dream I had two years earlier whilst living on the seafront in Kemptown, Brighton. In it, a similar thing happens; I am standing on the pebbly beach in front of my flat at low tide, the sun glinting on the water, and looking up I see a wave the height of a sizeable mountain, travelling straight and fast towards me. I wake up just before it hits. A familiar, momentary pang of sharp emotional pain in my chest, which has come and gone regularly since this dream, when I have contemplated what it would be like to lose my mother, now flushes through me. I shake it off and smile at her, tucking into the food. It is delicious; it tastes of love and many hours of slow simmering.

Everyone moves on to the next dish, and then my mother turns the conversation to the political news from Iran that week; her main subject of interest and passion. There is unrest brewing in Tehran again. 'It's that Khatami, the so-called reformist, we believed in him for a while, but he has done nothing he promised to – nothing really! Just smiling and nodding like a friendly fool! All those young people, those children of the revolution, they deserve so much more than this rubbish! Nothing is going to change at all, while we still have Khameini's so-called 'supreme leadership' calling all the shots, we need another revolution, I tell you children....'

****

It is late October, 2015. I am sitting on a couch in the Freud Museum, London, preparing for the opening performance of a night I have been curating with them called 'All About the Gift'. Around 100 people are now settling into what was once Freud's bedroom. As the last few people sit down, I feel their eyes on me, drawing me into the room more fully. I have a deep cold and a slight, lingering temperature. But this is an important moment and I tell myself, *Get present. This is happening. You aren't that ill.* The couch I am sitting on is a replica of Freud's original and is draped in an Iranian carpet, not unlike one on the floor of my mother's former bedroom.

The couch holds me gently as I sit with my notes and a fish-shaped object, a sculpture made out of card, wrapped and bound in yellow and emerald silk sari yarns, ready for a story and later, a collective, ritual performance. It is the first of many objects and stories that will be made – and eventually exchanged – by those present here, as I provoke them with my own story, inviting them to tell theirs and to make their own wrapped object as a gift - to be given away to a stranger here at the closing performance later.

One of the stories I am about to weave into this performance is from a well-thumbed book, which has countless corners turned over and lines highlighted in red pencil throughout. The book is called *The Gift: The Artist and Creativity in the Modern World* by Lewis Hyde.

The story I am sharing from it is the author's account of how the indigenous tribes of the North Pacific used a system of gift cycles to ensure a steady supply of salmon, during the time before white settlers commercialised fish farming. The tribes believed that all animals lived a parallel life – very similar to humans – and that the salmon lived together as a tribe in an underwater lodge, in human form.

Once a year they would transform themselves into fish bodies – wearing robes of salmon skin. They would swim to the river's edge to offer themselves up to the tribes in sacrifice, so that their land brothers would not go hungry during winter.

To acknowledge this great sacrifice, the first fish to appear would be greeted as an honoured guest, taken by a priest to be laid out in the direction of the land on an altar – to encourage the remaining salmon to swim upstream – and given delicate, ceremonial treatment. This included rituals and speeches evoking the continued abundance of the fish, and a welcome song by the whole tribe. The fish would then be divided up and eaten, with all its bones intact – in anticipation of being returned to the sea. The belief was that once the bones were slipped back in the water, the salmon would re-assemble itself, swim back to the lodge and become human again. This practice was crucial in ensuring an abundant salmon supply for all future winters.

I pause at the end of this section, offering up the fish in my hands for all to see and begin: 'Now let me tell you about my Mother…'

****

It is late December, 2004. You are on the phone to Ralph. He is giving you his account of what happened while they were away in Phuket. His voice is shaking, and you are trembling as you listen. Here is what he tells you. It is around 7.45am on Boxing Day, 2004. A beautiful, clear morning, golden white sand, deep blue sea and a completely clear sky. A picture postcard image. Ralph and your mother are two of only three early risers on this particular section of beach, awake after the previous night's Christmas partying at the hotel behind them. They are feeling relaxed, just taking in the beauty of the view ahead of them and the warm, light breeze. You imagine your mother wearing her flowery pink sarong and her orange and yellow bikini top. So at ease in her own body.

Suddenly, as they are walking along the edge of the water together, the atmosphere shifts. Everything darkens. They look out to sea and notice the waves pulling out from the beach rapidly, as they should do – but then not coming

157

back in again. An out breath, but no in breath. This sudden absence of water leaves hundreds of fish flipping around on the sand. Not far off there is a young boy taking easy pickings with a net and bucket. Your mother begins to instinctively move out towards the sea, picking up the fish, and trying to return them to the water.

When Ralph tells you this he almost laughs, but you hear a brief sob releasing in between his words: 'So typical of your mother! Always to the rescue....' As she tries to move, she steps barefoot onto some kind of ray fish in one of the shallow pools exposed by the absent wave, gets stung and cries out. Ralph suggests they turn back and get it treated at the hotel. 'No, I'll be fine, honestly,' she says, 'You go back and I'll follow you darling, I'll be there in a minute.' He turns around and starts heading back up the beach, towards their hotel high up on the hill. At that precise moment, the force of one of the strongest tsunamis ever experienced in history hits that entire coastline – and far beyond.

Ralph tells you that he remembers going under the water, quickly re-emerging, then grabbing and clinging onto a giant piece of wooden debris. As he is floating along, a boy perched high up on a rooftop ahead shouts at him and points back to a second wave rushing in. He manages to hoist himself onto the rooftop and stay above the level of the wave, crying out your mother's name 'Parvin!! Parvin!' over and over again. Silence. After a few hours, he is rescued and taken to a nearby hospital, a school repurposed for the crisis. Hundreds of pine needles are lodged into the soles of his feet. It takes weeks – and copious amounts of arnica administered by the hospital – for them to be extracted.

He pauses at the end of the phone call, and tells you in a tender but definite tone that it is impossible that your mother will now be found alive. 'I tell you, no one – especially a weak swimmer like your mother, god bless her – could have survived that. I'm sorry. I know it's not what you want to hear.'

At this point you don't believe him, you just go quiet and feel your eyes welling up with scorching, hot tears and a contracting sensation in your chest. There are a number of stories still coming out of survivors in far flung places and your mother seems to have had supernatural powers of survival up to this point – including car crashes and cancer scares – so you just cannot accept she is definitively gone. She had even arranged which days of the week she would be available to take the baby once she was old enough to be separated from you. The image of her washing up alive on a nearby island and nursing wounded people, smiling and chatting away, is still what you are clinging to. You put the phone down and keep hoping.

****

It is late February, 2005. Here I am, standing around a glass dining table in south London with my aunt, brothers, sisters, husband and Iranian cousins. My husband is holding our daughter Delaram, dozing on his shoulder. The table is covered with three different Iranian stews, a small glass bowl of *torshi* – handmade Iranian pickles – and a large cake of crisped up white rice which my cousin Shayesteh has just brought in. Everyone is strangely quiet as they help themselves to the food. Not the usual chat, excitement or delight. Most of these dishes are the food I have defrosted and brought from my own freezer; dishes made by my mother, love kept on ice for us. And, at the centre, two other dishes found in her home freezer which I brought back after starting to empty out her flat with my sister. One of them is a white fish dish from Southern Iran called *ghalieh mahi*, cooked in tamarind, fenugreek, coriander, garlic, turmeric, with a hint of curry. It was a new dish that I started craving for again straight after she made it for me the first time, it was so comforting and nourishing. My mother carefully showed me how to make it, writing down her extra tips and slipping the paper into her tiny, battered Persian Cookbook she gave me, which started to fall apart once she left; the ancient binding losing its elasticity, its pages starting to shed all over the kitchen, like a distressed animal.

Everyone in the room is sitting eating, at the table or on the sofa. I sit looking at the full plate of food on the glass table in front of me. The smells make my mouth water, but my eyes are stinging from trying to hold back my tears. I remember my mother stating many times that when she died, her wish was for there to be no crying, just celebration and drinking champagne in her honour. This now seems like a completely unfair – almost outrageous – request, given the sudden nature of her death, but I share this wish with everyone (though she seems to have informed them all of her wish already, as if pre-empting this moment, always and still one step ahead of us). Nevertheless, we all attempt to obey orders and wear a cheerful face, as my cousin Rostam fills each glass with the fizzing drink.

But a renewed sense of shock is filling the air. I don't have an appetite for anything at all. I just want to lie down, be alone and sleep – and not wake up for a long time. Perhaps never. There is a silent pause in the room. It seems to last for half an hour, but in reality, it's probably only five minutes.

Then, just for a split second, I think I can hear her, my mother, slightly impatiently but lovingly insisting *Come on, eat darlings, it will get cold!* I concede and take a spoonful of the spicy fish stew and a helping of fluffy, warm, buttery rice to go with it. I look up and see everyone else doing the same. As soon as the food hits my mouth, an immediate feeling of pleasure, comfort and longing surges through my body. I see eyes closing and smiles of satisfaction all around. My spine relaxes and my breath slows in a moment of relief. Everyone raises a glass. 'To Parvin!! To aunty! To mum!'

Hidden Sussex Contributors

http://writingourlegacy.org.uk/writers-artists/writers/

Georgina Aboud – Grow
Georgina Aboud is of Lebanese and Anglo-Irish heritage. She is writer and teacher and lives in Brighton.

Jenny Arach – Brighton Beach, At Home with the Queen
I'm both English and East African. I grew up in Brighton and Sussex as well as Uganda and Tanzania. I feel strong connections to all these places, which are entwined with my family life. I call all three places home, they all encapsulate my emotions and experiences and my poetry reflects these aspects of my life.

Sheila Auguste – Good Girl
Sheila Auguste moved to Brighton over 20 years ago, she moved from East London where she was born by way of St. Lucian parents. Some of who she is: a writer, a reader, a

walker, a fan of Zumba and yoga, a therapist, a feminist with a lovely husband.

Alinah Azadeh – The Unmarked Box, The Fish

Alinah Azadeh is a writer, artist, performer and social activist of mixed Iranian and English heritage. She has been making work for and with museums, galleries and diverse communities for over twenty years, including the National Portrait Gallery, South Bank Centre, Westminster Hall, Fabrica Gallery and Freud Museum, as well as internationally.

Priti Barua – Murmurations of Starlings

Priti Barua is passionate about nursing, teaching, and being a mum, using her remaining time to write. Currently she is editing her memoir arising from an extraordinary, exotic family history, entitled, In God's Kitchen. She has an MA in English and received a scholarship for a PhD in Creative Writing.

Bebb Burchell – A Snap Encounter

Bebb Burchell was born in 1948 in Cardiff, and attended secondary schools in North Wales and Derby. In 1966, she arrived at the new University of Sussex to read Developmental Psychology. Of the 3,000 undergraduates, there were three black students, two of were from the UK.

Josef Cabey – Pheasants

Josef Cabey was born in London moving to Brighton in 2003. He is primarily an artist who studied Graphic Design before going on to complete an MA in Library Information studies at University of Brighton where he is now also a part time librarian. The writing in this anthology is a reflection on his experience as a Londoner visiting the countryside and being fascinated by pheasants that for him came to symbolise that experience.

Suchi Chatterjee – Terracotta Cups, 1857-1947
Suchi Chatterjee is a Brighton-based playwright and journalist. She is a regular contributor to the renowned GSCENE magazine and Brighton & Hove Black History Project. Her play *Song of an African* is currently on in the Brighton Fringe and winner of the Irene Mensah Award.

Lisa Climie – My Mother Said
Born in Brighton, Lisa spent her early childhood in rural East Sussex. She has an MA in Biography and Creative Non-Fiction from UEA and, having moved to Hastings in 2015, is now perfecting her skills through New Writing South's Advanced Writing Workshops. Lisa specialises in writing memoirs and historical fiction.

Farah Edwards Khan – Martyrs on Parade
Farah Edwards Khan grew up in the central Indian city of Bhopal. Farah has formerly worked with writers such as Dominic Lapierre and Indra Sinha on novels about the 1984 Bhopal Gas Tragedy, which she witnessed as a child. Her stories focus on the lives of ordinary people in India.

Sally-Claire Fadelle – Turmeric Footprints
Sally-Claire Fadelle was born in West Sussex, the daughter of a Trinidadian father and an English mother. Sally writes poetry and prose and has worked as a storyteller and poet throughout Sussex. At this time, she is working on a novel

and has just completed the first year of an MA in Creative Writing at the University of Chichester.

Josephine Hall – There are More Shells Here
Josephine Hall is a writer and creator who grew up in Cornwall and enjoys experimenting and adventuring. She currently lives in Brighton and tends to write about creative approaches to travel, mental health and living lightly on the earth, as well as dabbling in poetry, song and memoir.

Jasmine Harris – Black Joy
Jasmine Harris is a secondary educator and published poet featured in Ink & Voices, Prometheus Dreaming, Rigorous, etc. Author of, I May Have Been In My Feelings, focuses her writing on identity, relationships, and societal climate. Harris frequently quotes her inspirations as Maya Angelou, Ntozake Shange, and Tupac Shakur.

Maggie Harris – Of Words, The Hastings Line, as Was, Rye
Maggie Harris is a Guyana-born writer living in Kent, Winner of the Guyana Prize for Literature 2000 and 2014 and Regional Winner of The Commonwealth Short Story Prize 2014.

L Oluwafemi Hughes Jonas – Beyond Borders
L Oluwafemi Hughes Jonas is British born of Nigerian and Indian parents. She grew up in Scotland and has lived in Brighton over 25 years. Femi is most at home among a community of friends and when close to nature on the South Downs Way. She has survived and is working towards thriving as a writer, poet, storyteller and a working facilitator of dreaming life, beyond the morass.

Dulani Kulasinghe – One Lesson
Dulani Kulasinghe was born in Colombo, Sri Lanka, raised in Albuquerque, New Mexico and now lives in Brighton with her family. She trained as a teacher and lawyer, became a mother and made children's theatre and has realised that, for her, storytelling is the thread that connects it all.

Georgina Parke – Wet Hair, The Doves of Moulsecoomb
Georgina Parke is a British poet and writer. She grew up by the Lincolnshire coast and has lived in Sussex for 18 years.

Annie Richardson – Weaving the Threads
Annie Richardson was born in a small village in East Sussex and now lives within 8 miles of her birthplace. She sees herself firstly as a black, mixed-heritage woman, proud wife, mother, grandmother and friend, however her day job is as a university lecturer on Early Childhood Education and Care.

Anaconda Sen – Whitehawk Woman
Anaconda Sen is a present day avatar of Whitehawk Woman. They both lived in Whitehawk - same place, different time. Anaconda's parents were born one in the north and one in the south of the globe, and Anaconda's own children were born in different earth again, north and west of the Sussex Weald.

Zaid S Sethi – Nine Years Old, Conrad
Zaid Sethi is a freelance writer and photographer, who has published two collections of short stories ('The End of the World and 'The Dream of Angels'), and two novels ('Faith, Hope & Love' and 'Paris'). He has also written two one-act plays: 'The Affair' and 'Lavender's Blue.'

Hayat Shehab – Unspeakable Seas, Beirut to Brighton Express

Born in Beirut to Lebanese and Syrian parents, Hayat Nezameddin Shehab has worked in teaching and law. Her family moved to London in the 1970s during the Lebanese civil war and she has since discovered that home exists somewhere in the complicated space between Brighton and Beirut.

Sonny Singh – Qismat

Sonny Singh was born in Brighton in 1976. His parents are Sikh Punjabi that moved to the UK from East Africa in the 1960's. He was bought up in Brighton and has lived in various places across the UK and Asia.

Nina Thaddeus – From Sindh to Sussex - My Mother's Memories

Nina Thaddeus is the author of 'I Love to See You Eat', a self-published reflection of her mother's Anglo Indian life from Karachi to Crawley. Born in Pakistan her family immigrated to the UK in the 1950's and settled in Sussex where Nina has spent most of her life.

Featured Artist

Ingrid Pollard, *Seaside Series*,1989

Ingrid Pollard is a photographer, media artist and researcher. She is a graduate of the London College of Printing and Derby University. Ingrid has developed a social practice concerned with representation, history and landscape with reference to race, difference and the materiality of lens based

media. Her work is included in numerous collections including the UK Arts Council and the Victoria & Albert Museum. She lives and works in London UK.
http://www.ingridpollard.com/

Partner Organisations

African Night Fever
African Night Fever showcases African music in the Brighton and the South East of London.
ebou@africannightfever.com / 07876 290187
https://www.africannightfever.co.uk/

Brighton & Hove Black History
Revealing Brighton and Hove's hidden past and helps local people get involved in mapping their own histories.
http://www.black-history.org.uk/

Crawley WORDfest
WORDfest is Crawley's first ever festival dedicated to celebrating words and writing in it's many forms.
info@wordfestcralwey.org
https://wordfestcrawley.org/

Creative Future
Creative Future work with talented artists & writers who lack opportunities due to mental health issues, disability or other social circumstances.
Community Base, 113 Queens Rd, Brighton, BN1 3XG
info@creativefuture.org.uk / 01273 234780
https://www.creativefuture.org.uk/

Diverse Crawley, Crawley

DIVERSE Crawley began in Summer 2017, launched as part of Crawley's 70th anniversary, to share and showcase the rich diversity of our town.

info@diversecrawley.org.uk / 07709821741

http://diversecrawley.org.uk/

Diversity Lewes

We celebrate our differences and create awareness on all discrimination.

tony@diversitylewes.org.uk /07796796449

http://www.diversitylewes.org.uk/

New Writing South

New Writing South serves writers from across southeast England. Whether you're an aspiring or established writer of novels, short stories, poems or plays, New Writing South is here to feed your creativity.

9 Jew St, Brighton BN1 1UT

hello@newwritingsouth.com / 01273 735353

https://newwritingsouth.com/

Shoreham Wordfest, Shoreham

Shoreham Wordfest is a celebration of words and ideas. Our aim is to support creativity for all ages and to inspire our audience with literature, drama, song and discussion.

general@shorehamwordfest.com / 07522 957691

https://shorehamwordfest.com/

This Too Is Real

An arts management and production company that supports the development of art and cultural work that promotes social cohesion, equality and diversity.
info@thistooisreal.co.uk / 07732 697290
https://www.thistooisreal.co.uk/

The Word Factory, London
London's Word Factory is the national organisation for short story excellence. Run by writers, not for profit but for passion.
http://www.thewordfactory.tv/

Hidden Sussex BAME Directory

We've compiled a list of Sussex tourist sites, organisations, groups and local businesses that will appeal to people of colour and people interested in diverse culture and heritage.
http://writingourlegacy.org.uk/whats-on/projects/sussex-bame-directory/

About Writing Our Legacy

Writing Our Legacy aims to raise awareness of the contributions of Black and Ethnic Minority (BME) writers, poets, playwrights and authors born, living or connected to Sussex and the South East.

Community Base, 113 Queens Road, Brighton BN13XG
info@writingourlegacy.org.uk | 07732 697290
http://writingourlegacy.org.uk/
Twitter: @BHwritinglegacy | Facebook: WritingOurLegacy
Instagram: WritingOurLegacy

SEAS (Socially Engaged Art Salon) is a space for exhibitions, events, workshops & an artist residencies that centres on socially & politically engaged art practices & themes.
Based at the B.MECP, the centre for Black & Monitory Ethnic (BME) communities & Directed by Dr. Gil Mualem-Doron, SEAS is a beacon for social art in Brighton & the south-east England.

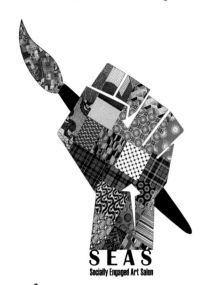

SEAS
Socially Engaged Art Salon

Proposals for group or solo exhibitions, workshops & events are welcomed!
seasbrighton@gmail.com
www.seasbrighton.com

SEAS / B.MECP, 10/A Fleet St. Brighton BN1 4ZE

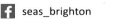 seas_brighton   seas_brighton   @brighton_seas

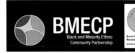   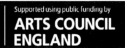

Lightning Source UK Ltd.
Milton Keynes UK
UKHW021353040321
379783UK00007B/15

Sink or Swim

*Catholicism in Sixties Britain
through John Ryan's Cartoons*

— ALANA HARRIS & ISABEL RYAN —

Sacristy
Press

Sacristy Press
PO Box 612, Durham, DH1 9HT

www.sacristy.co.uk

First published in 2020 by Sacristy Press, Durham

Sacristy Limited, registered in England & Wales, number 7565667

British Library Cataloguing-in-Publication Data
A catalogue record for the book is available from the British Library

Paperback ISBN 978-1-78959-138-5
Hardback ISBN 978-1-78959-139-2

To Priscilla Ryan

1927 ~ 2020

*John Ryan's wife, dedicated supporter
and creative assistant*

Contents

Foreword

To be asked to write a foreword to this wonderful book of John Ryan's cartoons is more than an honour. It is also an invitation to take a walk down Nostalgia Avenue. As a cartoonist, his work was by no means confined to the pages of the *Catholic Herald*, but it was in those pages that I met him in 1964. I felt an immediate bond. He had his own views about changes in our Church, with some of which he was out of sympathy. He could poke gentle fun at situations and people he found funny, but cruelty or sarcasm was just not in his nature. He wasn't blind to absurdities or pretensions, especially when they came from clergy at whatever level. His portly self-important and slightly sinister Cardinal Grotti is more fun than sign of animosity. But the laity too are teased for their division into progressives and conservatives.

The collection in this book has to be selective. John must have produced thousands of cartoons in his working life. When he began with the *Catholic Herald*, the Second Vatican Council was well under way and soon came *Humanae Vitae* and the Birth Control controversy. The contemporary background was that of a very self-confident Church and a firmly authoritarian one.

Cartoon 3 on page 16 sums up very well some of the turmoil of that time. A lot of heated bishops swimming about in confusion. Another good example is cartoon 11 on page 24 as a plump and bald parish priest tells a couple of clearly irritated women church cleaners "Good news for you, ladies! . . . Women should be ever more closely associated with church structures." Many of them are still waiting.

John was astute when it came to depicting the gap between the "ordinary faithful" and what was going on at the Vatican level. I love cartoon 29 on page 48 where a reporter is questioning a mother with a pram, surrounded by her brood of children. She answers: "Encyclical? Bless you, I don't have time to read Encyclicals . . . "

At the end comes a great photo of a laughing John and his smiling wife meeting Cardinal Hume—all with glasses of something nice in hand. That is how I would like to remember him. A warm, generous, humorous and very talented family man who had great affection for his Church, warts and all.

Bruce Kent
London, October 2020

Acknowledgements

This collection stems from an exhibition which ran at Ushaw College, Durham (September–December 2018) and at the Maughan Library, Chancery Lane, London (January–April 2019) with funding from the Faculty of Arts and Humanities and the Department of History at King's College London.

We would like to thank the *Catholic Herald* and The Estate of John Ryan for permission to use illustrations and Priscilla Ryan and Nick MacRae for the loan of artworks and photographs, and to Priscilla Ryan for her generous funding contribution to the exhibition display. We also thank the Catholic Record Society for their support of the exhibition and of the publication of this book.

For unfailing encouragement and sometimes immensely practical help—as removalists, sommeliers, workshop facilitators, photographers, tour guides—the authors would like to thank Nick, Lucy, Tim and Sebastian.

"*If* Catholic Herald *readers are shocked to realize that the artist who has been irritating or even occasionally entertaining them for so long is in fact one whose work is mainly for children, I can only suggest in all humility that there is a passage in the Gospel to console them and me. For me it is a pleasure to draw from time to time for adults, and even occasionally to have to think seriously. Personally I regret many of the recent changes within the Church. But for a cartoonist in a Catholic newspaper it is undeniable that the last few years have been rich in opportunity!*"

John Ryan, 1971

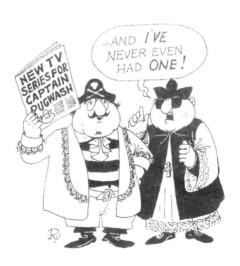

Charting the Territory: Compass Points

1923: *Stopes v. Sutherland* libel trial over contraception

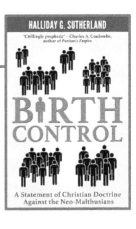

HALLIDAY G. SUTHERLAND

'Chillingly prophetic' – Charles A. Coulombe, author of *Puritan's Empire*.

B★RTH CONTROL

A Statement of Christian Doctrine Against the Neo-Malthusians

1923 ⟩ 1927 ⟩ 1930 ⟩ 1943 ⟩

1927: Pope Pius XI defines "Catholic Action" as the "participation of the laity in the apostolate of the hierarchy"

1943: Formation of the British Council of Churches by the Archbishop of Canterbury, William Temple

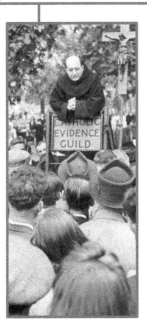

1930: Seventh Lambeth Conference, resolution 15 (contraception in marriage licit) and 61–72 on the Ministry of Women

1930: Pope Pius XI's Encyclical on Christian Marriage, *Casti Connubii*

1943: Foundation of the English Liturgical Society, later the Vernacular Society of Great Britain (1952 onwards)

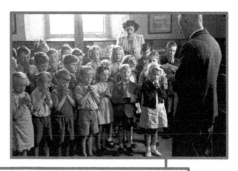

1944: (Butler) *Education Act*, establishing the tripartite education system, with special arrangements for faith schools (and religious instruction)

1944 ⟩ 1946 ⟩ 1950 ⟩ 1951 ⟩

1946: Establishment of the Catholic Marriage Advisory Council, with State funding from 1948

1950: 100th anniversary of the Restoration of the Hierarchy of England and Wales

1951: Pope Pius XII sanctions the use of the infertile period (rhythm method)

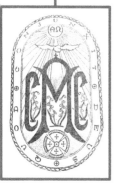

1950: Declaration of the Dogma of the Assumption

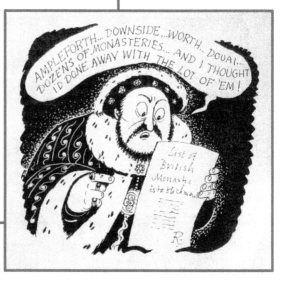

4

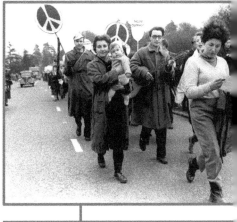

1957: Establishment of the Campaign for Nuclear Disarmament

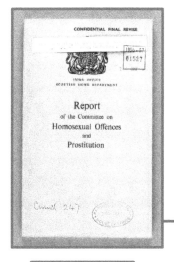

1957: Wolfenden Report on Homosexual Offences and Prostitution

1955: War in Vietnam until 1975

1955 〉 1956 〉 1957 〉 1958 〉

1956: Pope Pius XII's Encyclical on the Sacred Heart, *Haurietis Aquas*

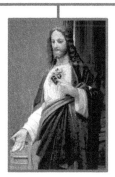

1958: 100th anniversary of the Marian apparitions at Lourdes

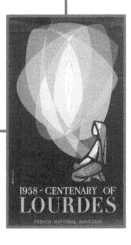

1958 - CENTENARY OF
LOURDES
FRENCH NATIONAL RAILROADS

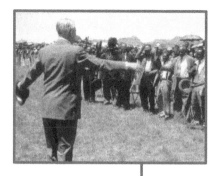

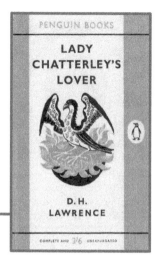

1960: Harold Macmillan's "Winds of Change" speech, Cape Town

1960: *R v. Penguin Books*, prosecution of D. H. Lawrence's *Lady Chatterley's Lover* on the grounds of obscenity

1960: *Betting and Gaming Act*, legalizing gambling

1961: Birth control pill available on the NHS for the first time to married women

1959 ⟩ 1960 ⟩ 1961 ⟩ 1962 ⟩

1959: Pope John XXIII gives notice of his intention to convene the Second Vatican Council

1962: Second Vatican Council opens in Rome

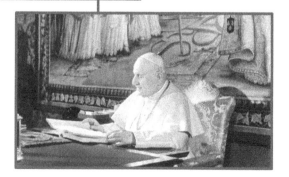

1963: President John F. Kennedy is assassinated in Dallas, USA

1964: Gwynne Evans and Peter Allen, last men hanged in Britain, resulting in the *Murder Act 1965*

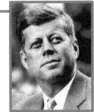

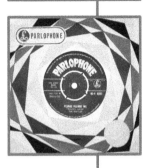

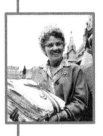

1963: "Please Please Me" first studio album is released by The Beatles

1964: Mary Whitehouse inaugurates her "Clean-up TV" campaign

1963

1964

1963: Publication by the Anglican Bishop of Woolwich, John A. T. Robinson, of *Honest to God*

1964: Introduction of some English into parts of the Mass in England and Wales

1964: John Ryan draws his first cartoon for the *Catholic Herald*

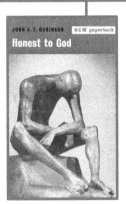

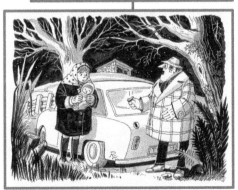

1963: Publication of John Rock's *The Time Has Come: A Catholic Doctor's Proposals to End the Battle over Birth Control*

1967: *Abortion Act* legalized abortion (on certain grounds) and regulated its provision through the NHS

1967: *Sexual Offences Act*, decriminalizing homosexuality, in private, between two men over the age of 21

1967–1970: Nigerian Civil War, also known as Biafran War

1968: Conservative MP for Wolverhampton, Enoch Powell's "Rivers of Blood" speech

1968: *Theatres Act* abolished censorship of the stage by the Lord Chamberlain's Office

1968: Start of "The Troubles" sectarian war in Northern Ireland, which continued for several decades

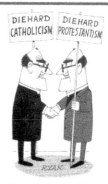

Together, we could destroy so much!

1967   1968

1968: Pope Paul VI's Encyclical, *Humanae Vitae*, prohibiting the use of artificial contraception

1967: Herbert McCabe OP is suspended temporarily from editorship of *New Blackfriars* magazine

1967: Charles Davis—prominent theologian and priest—leaves the Church and later marries

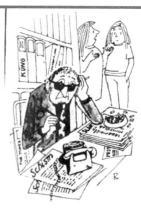

"Poor Charles . . . if only *somebody* would ask him to sign *something* . . . !"

1969: *Divorce Reform Act*, allowing for 'no fault' divorce after irretrievable breakdown

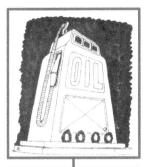

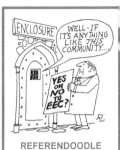

REFERENDOODLE

1973 – Oil Crisis: OPEC proclaims an oil embargo and oil prices soar

1973: Britain joins the European Economic Community

1969 ⟩ 1970 ⟩ 1971 ⟩ 1973

1969: Establishment of the Anglican-Roman Catholic International Commission (ARCIC)

1971: "Agatha Christie Indult", issued by Pope Paul VI, allowing the use of the (1965) Tridentine Mass

1970: Motu Proprio *Mysterii Paschalis*, which reorganized the Saints' Calendar, resulting in the removal of St Christopher and other non-historically verifiable cultus

1970: Canonization of the 40 Martyrs of England and Wales

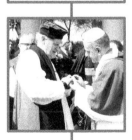

1969: Pope Paul VI's Apostolic Constitution, *Missale Romanum*, which enshrined the vernacular

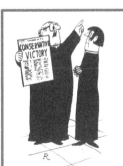

"Turn the altar round, bring me my Missale Romanum and GET YOUR HAIR CUT!"

1971: Nationwide Festival of Light

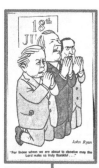

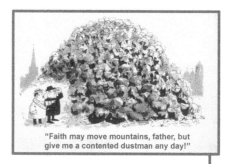

"Faith may move mountains, father, but give me a contented dustman any day!"

1974: General Election (Harold Wilson, Edward Heath and Jeremy Thorpe)

1975: *Referendum Act*, confirming Britain's continued membership of the EEC

1978-79: "Winter of Discontent"—widespread strikes in the public sector trade unions over pay and conditions

1974 ⟩ 1975 ⟩ 1976 ⟩ 1978

1976: Benedictine monk Basil Hume is chosen as new Archbishop of Westminster

1978: John Paul II's election (and visit to Ireland)

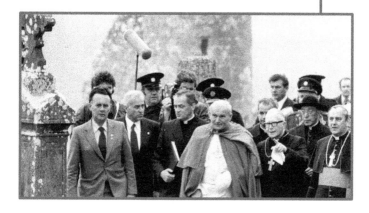

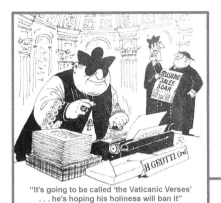

"It's going to be called 'the Vaticanic Verses' . . . he's hoping his holiness will ban it"

1988: The *Satanic Verses* controversy (or Rushdie affair)

1979 〉 1980 〉 1982 〉 1988

1982: First Papal Visit to Britain since the Reformation

1980: National Pastoral Congress, Liverpool

1979: Movement for the Ordination of Women (Church of England) formed

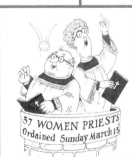

37 WOMEN PRIESTS Ordained Sunday March 15

REVEREND SPRAT IS SHORT & FAT, HIS WIFE IS TALL AND LEAN; WITH *HER* ORDAINED THEY NICELY FIT THE 'HIGH' & 'LOW' CHURCH SCENE.

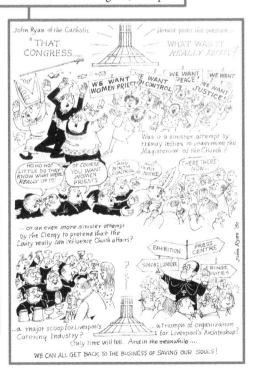

CHAPTER 1

The Barque of St Peter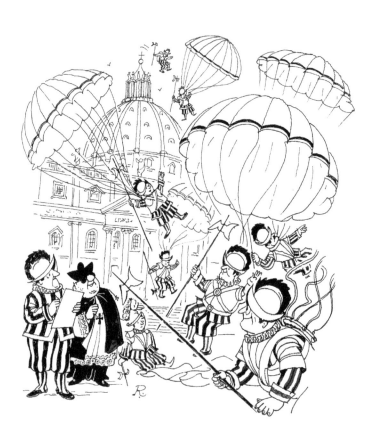

The Catholic Church on the cusp of the 1960s

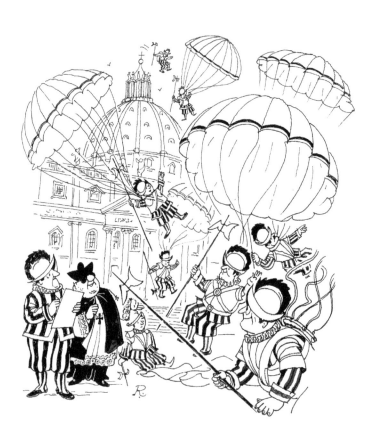

When Pope John XXIII convened the Second Vatican Council (also known as Vatican II) on 25 January 1959, few could anticipate the monumental changes it would inaugurate through its sixteen foundational documents.

Tasked with considering "the condition and updating (*aggiornamento*) of the Church", particularly after the dislocations of World War II, this assembly of over 2,000 bishops and an entourage of religious observers and news reporters met over four sessions at St Peter's Basilica in Rome from 1962–65. [2]

It was an unprecedented media event—warranting front-page commentary and intensive coverage from print and television news outlets around the world. [3] John Ryan, under the auspices of the *Catholic Herald*, sketched these "doings in Rome" in September 1965. His (unpublished) humorous vignettes of prelates and laity, speeches, Roman sights [4] and spaghetti offer an alternative vision of the "everyday" Council; it complements the theological sparring of "progressives" and "traditionalists" narrated by others, [5] such as *The New Yorker* correspondent and Redemptorist priest Xavier Rynne.

In the years following, wranglings over the legacy of the Council and its "spirit" [6] continued to rage. [7] Flare-ups related to the reform of the curia [8] and canon law, [9] the writings of well-known theologians and their scrutiny by the CDF, [10] and the place of women within the Church. [11] These were encoded references to one's stance on the post-conciliar Church—the balance

between change and continuity. Echoes of these debates continue into the present.

In a British Catholic context, this played out particularly in attitudes to contraception, the "new morality", the authority of religious teaching and catechetics. This was epitomized through the controversial foundation and short-lived operation of Corpus Christi College, Westminster, [12] and calls for conciliarism, church renewal and greater lay ministry. [13]

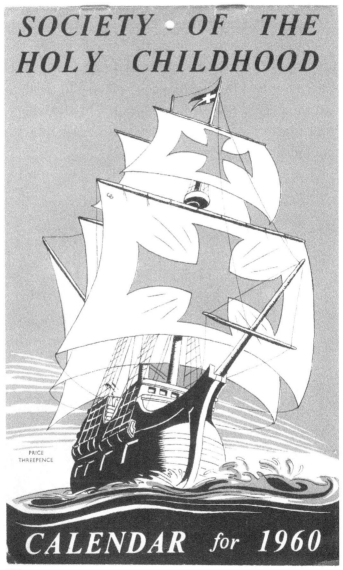

1

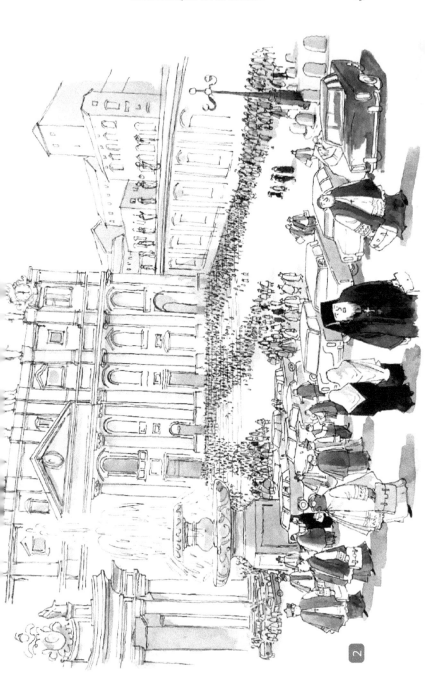

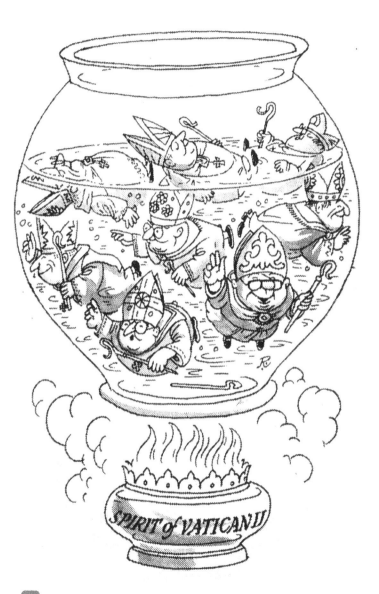

SPIRIT of VATICAN II

3

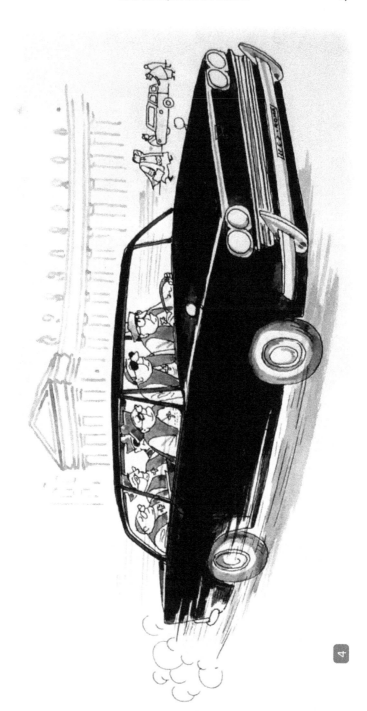

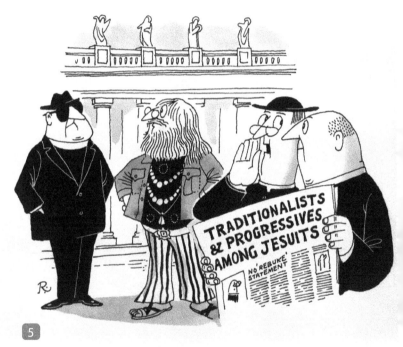

*"They really did try to resolve their differences;
at the start of the congregation they were
exactly the other way round!"*

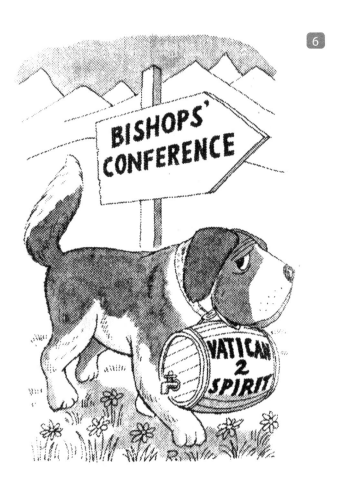

"*They can't all have given it up!*"

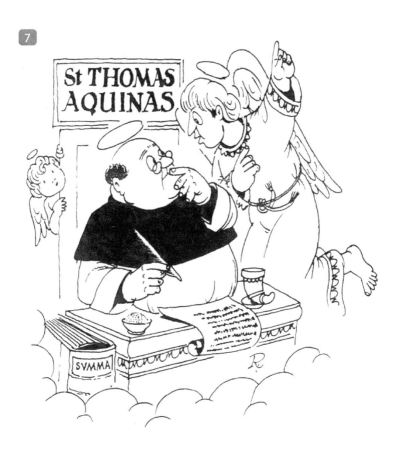

"You're wanted upstairs . . . He says He
can't follow the latest encyclical"

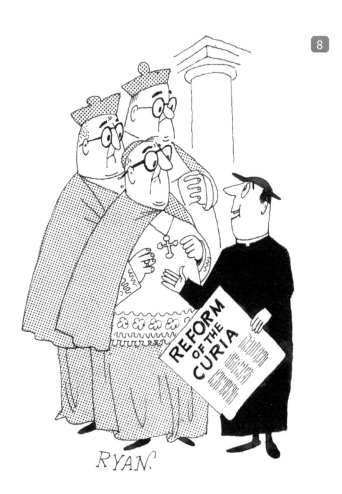

*At least they won't be able to say that
CURIAsity killed the CATholic Church!*

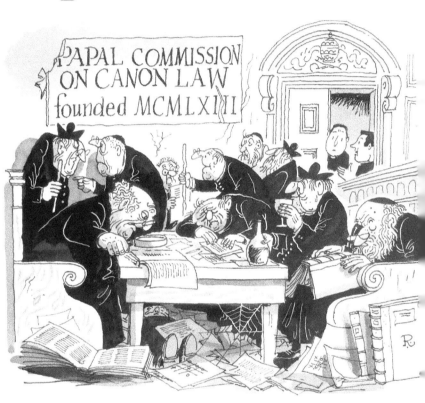

"One of the cleaners found them. It seems they've been here for about eighteen years!"

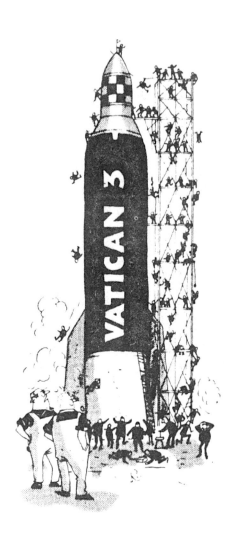

10

"If that baby blasts off . . . my name's Ottaviani!"

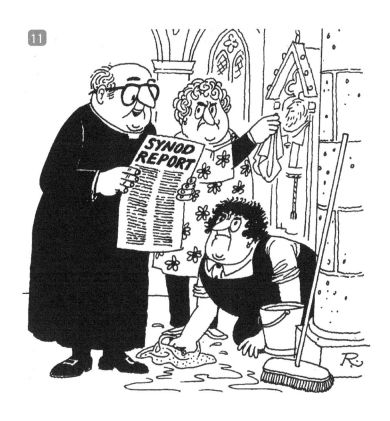

"Good news for you, ladies! It goes on
. . . 'Women should be ever more closely
associated with church structures'"

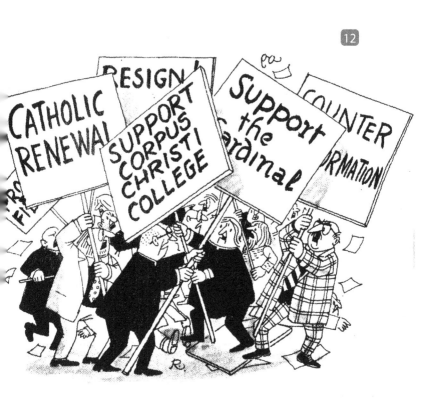

*Special prayers are offered this week
for Christian unity . . .*

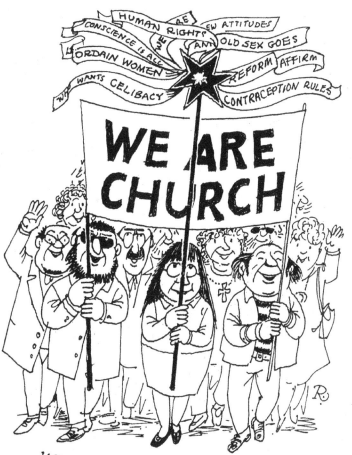

13

CHAPTER 2

Choppy Waters

Implementing the Second Vatican Council

The reforms inaugurated by Vatican II had different effects throughout the Catholic world. For the Catholic Church in England and Wales—a minority denomination of around 10 per cent of the population compared to the established Church of England—the legacy of Henry VIII's Reformation and the witness of the Elizabethan martyrs remained central and defining of Catholic identity four centuries later. Identification as a "recusant" (refusing) church, and attachment to material markers of difference—the Tridentine Latin Mass, 14 devotion to Mary and the Saints, the habits of nuns and women religious, 15 and polyphonic music 16—were all features of distinctiveness.

The movement from Latin to the vernacular (in our context, English) 17 was particularly contested in Britain from 1964–70. This took the form of the lay-led Latin Mass Society, which campaigned against any "capitulation to Cranmer", 18 "betrayal of the 40 martyrs" and a fresh "stripping of the altars". 19 Traditionalists

decried the reorientation of the altar and new styles of music. 20 A more minimalist church architectural aesthetic became fashionable, 21 necessitating the removal of many statues and sometimes the relocation of the tabernacle.

In 1971, a number of prominent Catholics (and non-Catholics too), worried about the loss of cultural heritage inherent in an ancient Christian ritual, wrote to Pope Paul VI to seek permission for continued use of the Latin Mass. 22 The so-called "Agatha Christie" 23 indult—unique before a universal imprimatur was granted in 1984 24A 24B—extended permission for the occasional celebration of the liturgy in Latin.

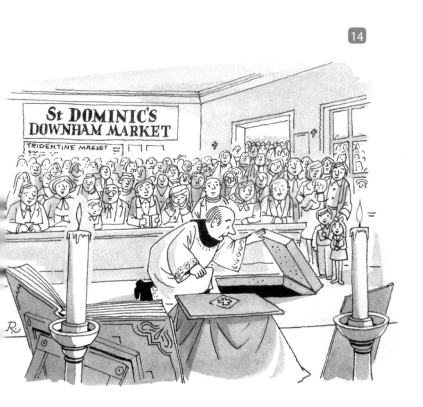

"*You can come out father . . . His Lordship's gone . . .*"

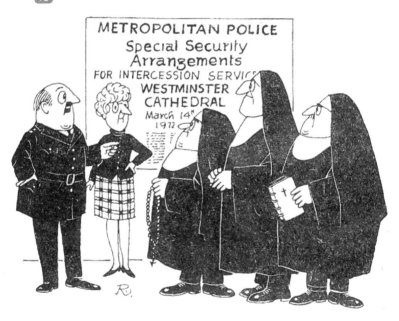

"*Your disguises are excellent, gentlemen—but, as reverend mother here points out, somewhat outdated!*"

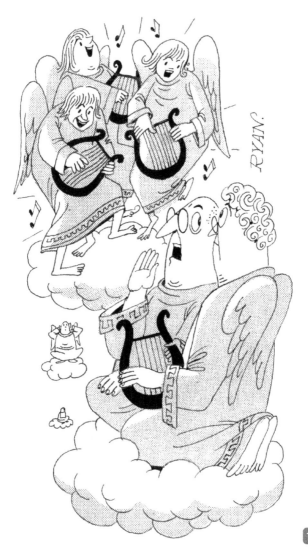

"*It all started with that correspondence on religious music in the* Catholic Herald!*"*

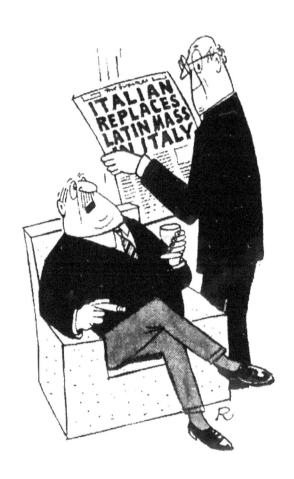

Scandalous! The Mass in a foreign language . . .

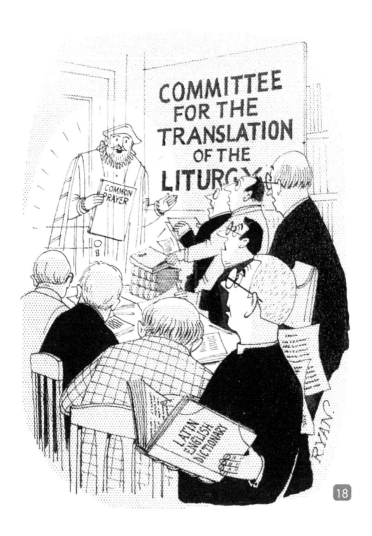

*"My name's Cranmer . . . I wondered if
I might be of any assistance . . . ?"*

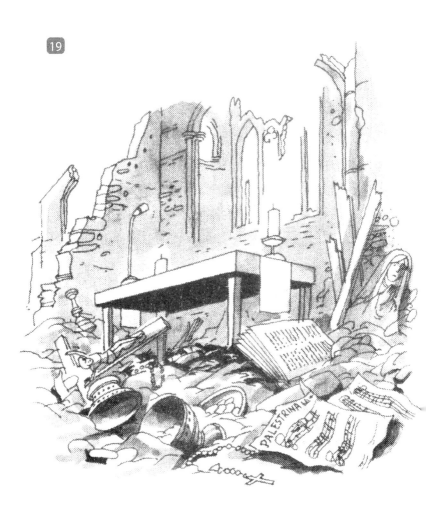

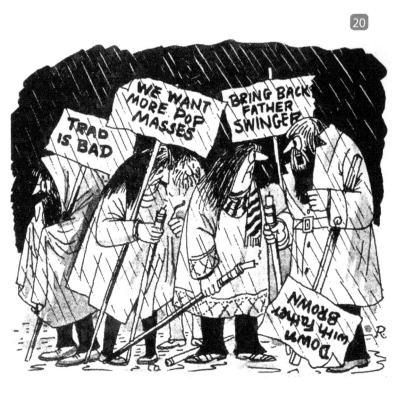

"And whose bright idea was it to hold a torchlit protest outside the presbytery on a March evening in England!"

21

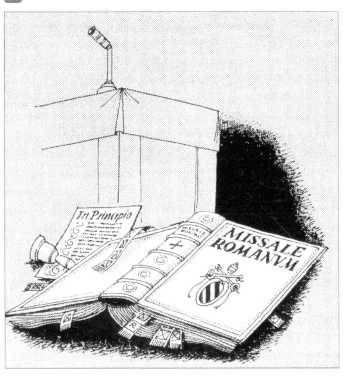

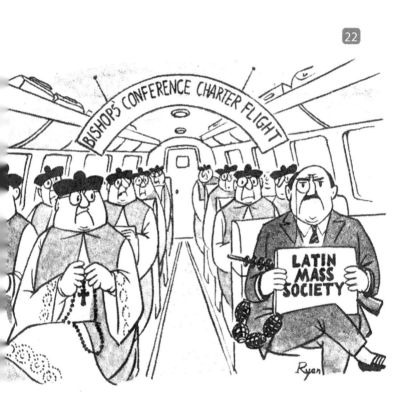

"Some call it 'putting the clock back' . . . Others call it 'returning to God's time' . . . "

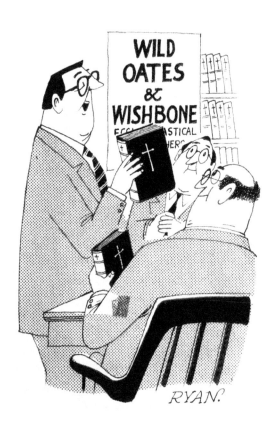

*"Intercontinental Missal" would be out of date . . .
"Anti-Missal Missal" is too competitive . . . How
about calling it the "Earth-to-Heaven" Missal?*

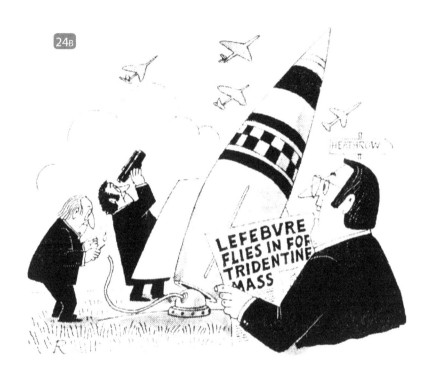

*"He's due any moment now! Watch
out for a Trident jet!"*

A Perfect Storm

The Humanae Vitae *Encyclical, 1968*

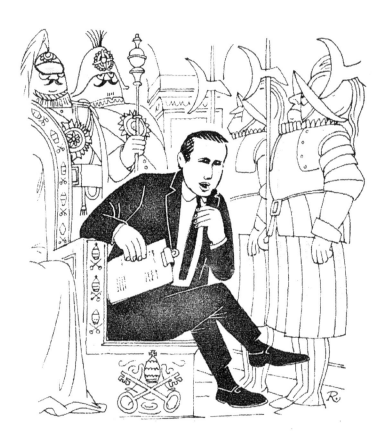

On 29 July 1968, Pope Paul VI's encyclical condemning the use of "artificial contraception" was promulgated, immediately provoking waves of outraged criticism and, in some cases, outright rebellion across the developed Catholic world. 25

This "crisis in the Church", as *The Tablet* dubbed it, was a long time brewing, given that the issue of the legitimacy of birth control (chiefly the contraceptive pill) within marriage was raised at the Council. In an attempt to defer—and diffuse—this issue, the Pope had referred the topic to a Vatican Commission of medico-moral and theological experts who recommended, as a majority in 1966, 26 that changes in the Church's position were possible and preferable.

When the papal adjudication (in the negative) came, hundreds of letters to the Catholic and mainstream Press, 27 and incessant coverage on television and radio, 28 conveyed the confusion and disappointment of many laywomen and men. For others, long adherents to the established teaching, there was relief at the welcome, counter-cultural intervention that the Pope's affirmation of the traditional position signalled. 29

Outraged reactions were common across Europe, but as a *Catholic Herald* leader adjudged, "the UK reaction [was] most intense". This was fuelled by the counter-position of the Church of England's support for family planning, the decision of the Macmillan government to provide the pill on the NHS, and the activism of a number of socially mobile, vociferous, and newly

university-educated Catholics. Pray-ins, large-scale conferences, petitions to the press (by clergy and laity) and an "ad hoc" committee **30** to coordinate protest and support dissenting priests **31** (or those seeking laicization) **32** were features of the summer of 1968 in Catholic Britain. **33**

The *Catholic Herald* was in the eye of the storm during these months, as its editor, Desmond Albrow, had criticized the papal ruling as "not the last word". Additionally, regular *Catholic Herald* columnist (and Conservative MP) Norman St John-Stevas was at the forefront of opposition in print, on television and through lay organizational action. John Ryan's stance on the controversy, as seen through his cartoons, was milder, more ambivalent, **34** and gently ironic. **35**

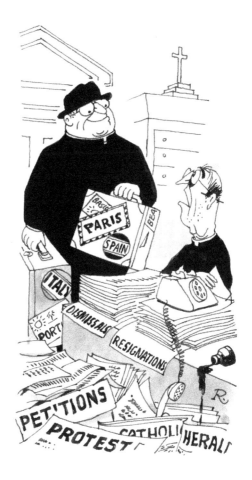

25

"*Well, YES, my Lord . . . since you ask . . . there HAVE been one or two little matters . . .*"

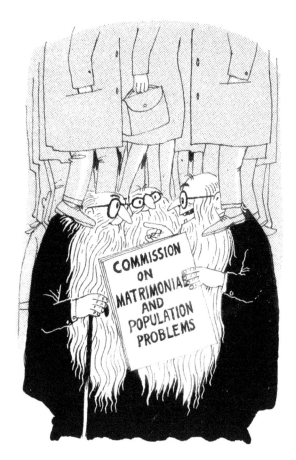

"And now . . . for the Report . . . !"

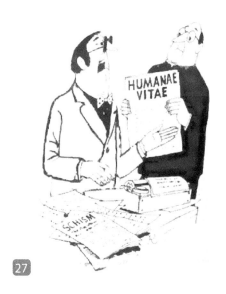

27

*"Read it? I'm a busy man, father . . .
I have to write about it . . . "*

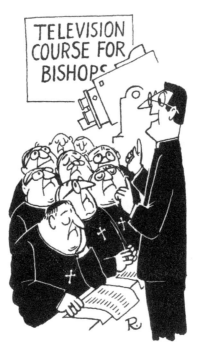

"*My ideal is to give you all an image somewhere between Frost, Muggeridge, Heenan, and Mick Jagger.*"

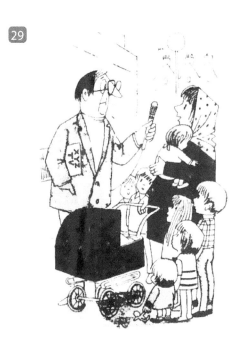

*"Encyclical? Bless you, I don't have
time to read Encyclicals . . . "*

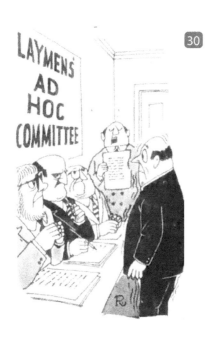

"That he did publicly recite and incite the recitation of the rosary, and refer in terms of eulogy to the Council of Trent . . . "

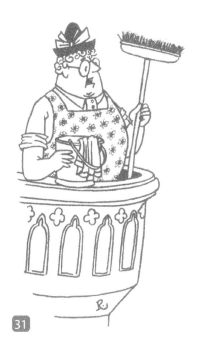

31

"*The rector 'avin' resigned 'cos the Cardinal's gone too far and the curate 'avin' resigned 'cos 'e ain't gone far enough . . . you'd best all sing 'Faith of our fathers' and 'op it 'ome!*"

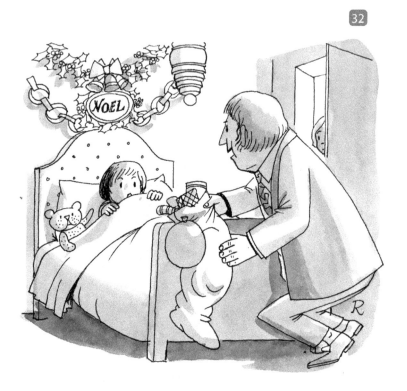

*"Actually son – Father Christmas has
laicised himself this year . . . "*

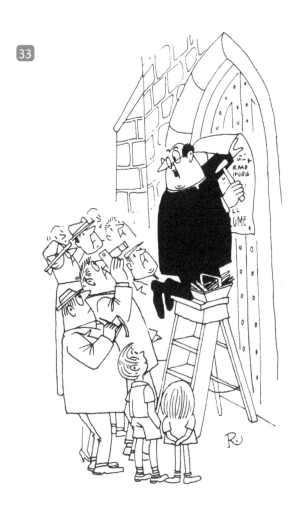

"No, gentlemen, I am not *a second Luther, and this is
merely a notice about the Autumn church bazaar!"*

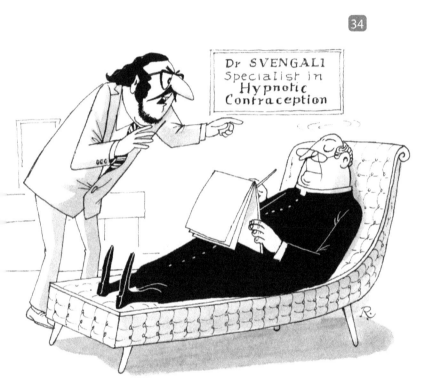

"Deeply asleep, Fr Basso. And now write:- 'This method may prove highly acceptable to the Catholic Church' . . . and add my name and address!"

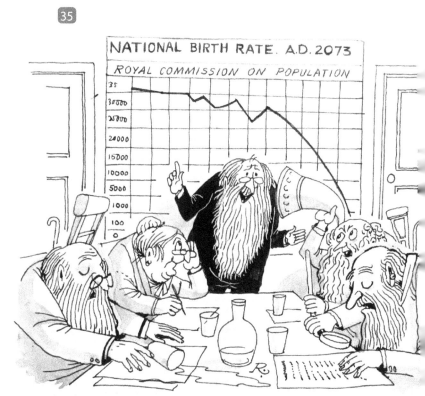

"So now we have only to convert the remaining
schools into geriatric wards and the creches into
mortuaries and our task is at an end . . . "

CHAPTER 4

Swimming Against the Tide

The Permissive Society and her Enemies

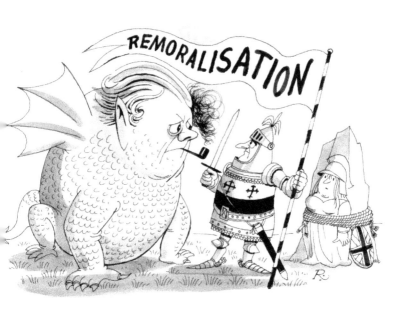

The 1960s was a decade of rapid social, cultural and religious change, albeit with clear and often unacknowledged roots in the years between the two World Wars. The Catholic Church, alongside other traditional institutions, was not immune from demands for change. Pope John XXIII, when opening the Second Vatican Council in October 1962, signalled his hope that it would "bring the Church up-to-date" where required. He urged the Council Fathers to disregard the pessimism of the "prophets of doom" who prognosticated that "the modern world is lost in a morass of prevarication and ruin".

There were some within the churches who embraced these "signs of the times", seeking to update the gospel message for "modern man" and to draw creatively upon the theological innovations prompted by the horrors of Hiroshima and the "Death of God" in the concentration camps. John Robinson, the Bishop of Woolwich, synthesized this new theology in his book *Honest to God* (1963). It was an unexpected bestseller and his previous role as witness for the defence in the *Lady Chatterley's Lover* trial confirmed him, and other Anglican "Southbank Theologians", as spokespeople for the "new morality" and the cardinal virtue of "love". 36

Yet some Britons, perhaps epitomized by the conservative journalist and Christian convert Malcolm Muggeridge, were disturbed by the raft of so-called "permissive" legislation across the decade: decriminalization of homosexuality and abortion, the

outlawing of capital punishment and the liberalization of the laws on censorship, 37 blasphemy and gambling. 38A 38B 38C Others, such as an advisory group appointed by the Archbishop of Canterbury to investigate "divorce law for contemporary society", supported change in the *Putting Asunder* report which formed the basis for liberalization in 1969. 39

The Catholic Church in England, in its stance on the traditional family, 40 non-contraceptive marital sexuality and fervent opposition to abortion, 41 was often associated with those who lamented change as opening the floodgates to immorality and promiscuity. 42 Articulated through movements such as Mary Whitehouse's "Clean-up TV" campaign and the Festival of Light (1971), this contested moral landscape was a favourite topic for John Ryan's cartoons.

Ryan's protagonists, especially an overweight and complacent *Britannia*, explored the ambiguities inherent in the decline in Britain's imperial power and the liberalizing impulses of the decade (and beyond). Ryan humorously parodied the sometimes contradictory outcomes of freedom of expression, personal autonomy, individualism and growing affluence alongside deindustrialization, strikes and increasing unemployment. 43

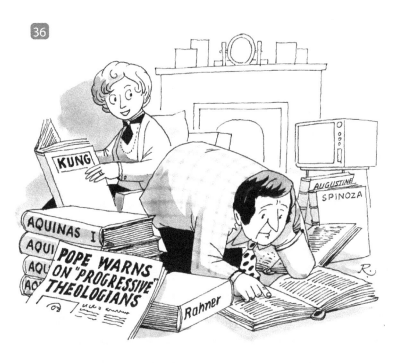

"*But something Küng says here makes
me think that perhaps we could go to the
Jones' wife-swapping party . . .*"

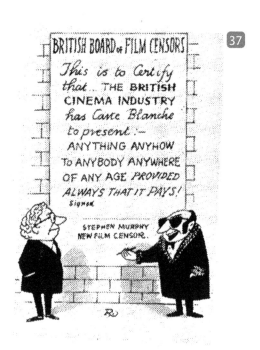

"Just one signature, Mr Murphy . . . and you can leave the rest to us . . . "

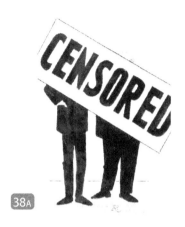

38ᴀ

"It may be a bad cartoon but it's in frightfully good taste"

38ʙ

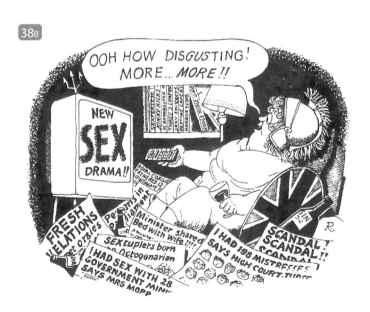

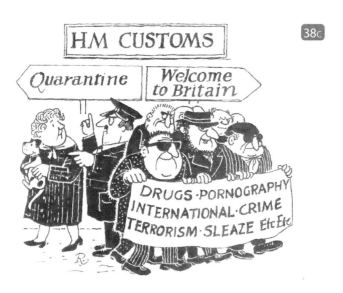

38c

Why only pets?

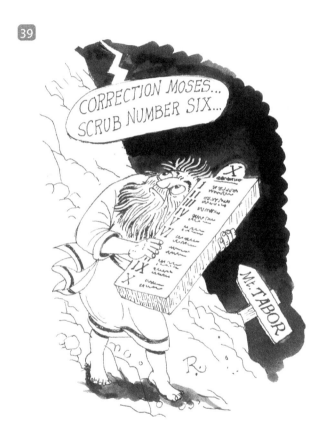

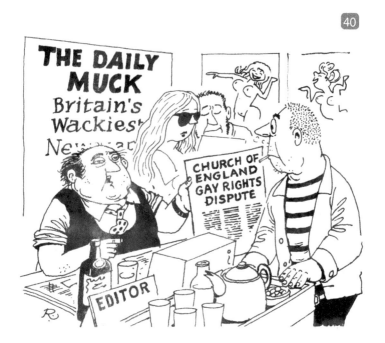

"See what you can rake up, Fred. Its your turn to be religious correspondent today . . . "

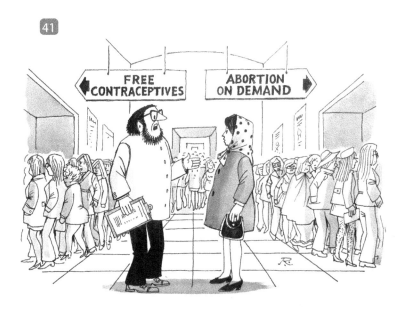

"*Maternity . . . ? They closed down weeks ago
. . . You can't have everything, y'know*"

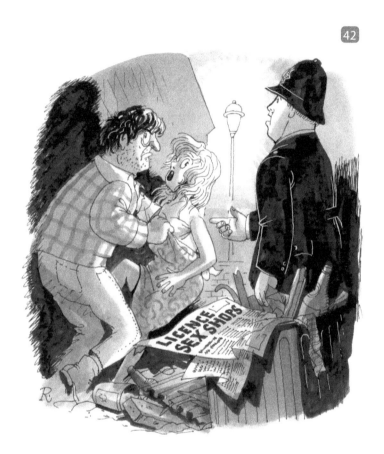

"Excuse me sir, may I see your licence . . . "

43

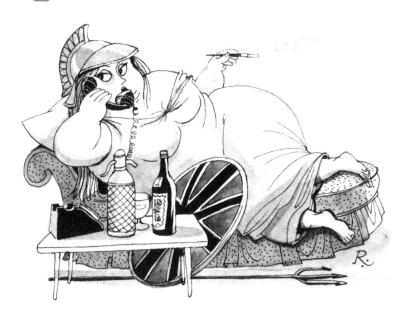

" . . . Just don't know what life's coming to
. . . blackouts on the telly and the doctors
cutting off the free contraceptives . . . "

CHAPTER 5

"Withdrawing Roar of the Sea of Faith"?

Secularization

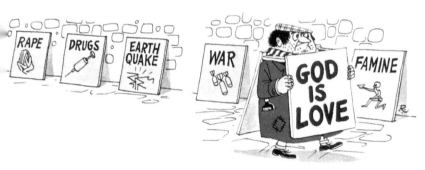

Evaluating these transformations, liberal theologians and sociologists of religion in the Sixties proclaimed "the secular city" 44 and the advent of "man come of age". For others—clergy and laity alike—the changes in the religious landscape of Britain were a portent of the churches' loss of institutional standing and the declining "public salience of religion". 45

Seemingly emblematic of such changes were the relaxation of the laws on censorship and blasphemy, giving rise to religious satire—such as Tom Lehrer's

1966 television performance of "The Vatican Rag" on *That was the Week that Was*. In a different vein, the gospel story was given an updated treatment in musicals like *Jesus Christ Superstar* (1970). 46 Following on from the Council's sanction in 1963, historical criticism of the Bible was condoned, 47 the penny catechism was jettisoned, and religious education increasingly drew on post-conciliar tenets and new, child-centred theories of education. 48 49

Moving into the 1960s, the Catholic Church in England and Wales had been confident and complacent—buoyed by remarkably high convert rates (doubtless powered by the prohibition on "mixed marriages") and impressive Mass attendances in performance of one's "Sunday obligation". These (institutional) markers of strength—which had differentiated twentieth-century Catholicism from the other Christian denominations—did not persist by the end of the decade. The use of the sacraments, especially confession, was falling; 50 there was a sharp drop off in conversions (perhaps linked to ecumenism), 51 and some were shocked by notable defections of clergy (to marry, or prompted by *Humanae Vitae* opposition). 52

Pessimistic headlines pronouncing fewer people in the pew 53 were taken as proof of secularization 54 and the "dechristianization" of British culture. 55 This was placed alongside the rise of new spiritualties 56 and the advent of real ethnic diversity and religious pluralism in decolonized Britain. 57 Some blamed the

Second Vatican Council—urging the episcopacy to "put the clock back". [58] John Ryan's cartoons surveyed all this territory. They were sanguine in recognizing that the diagnosis of decline was a recurrent concern for churchmen, [59] while calls for revival might give rise to new religious currents that were not always to everyone's taste. [60]

[44]

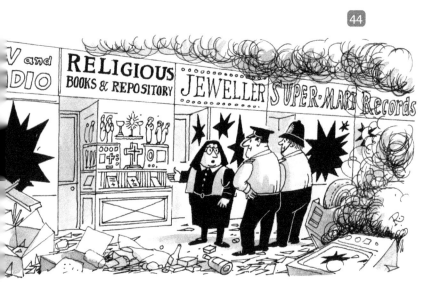

*"A miracle? . . . Or could it be
they're just not interested?"*

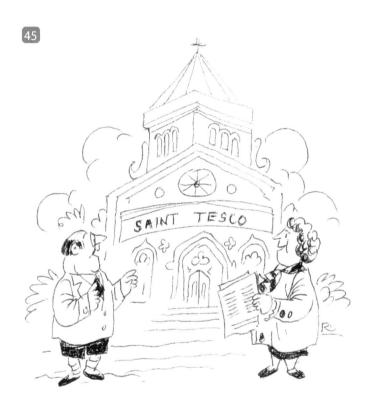

"*Very convenient . . . church and
supermarket all in one!*"

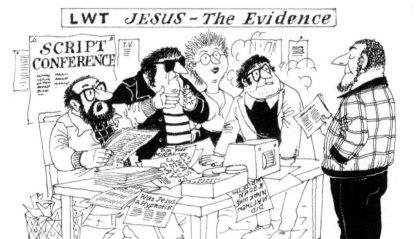

"Marvellous! Just when we've got a really juicy script going, Fred here proves the guy never existed!!"

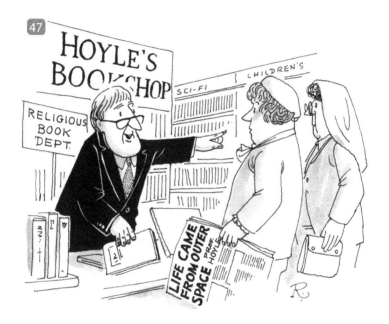

*"No, ladies . . . Bibles are now in
the <u>scientific</u> department"*

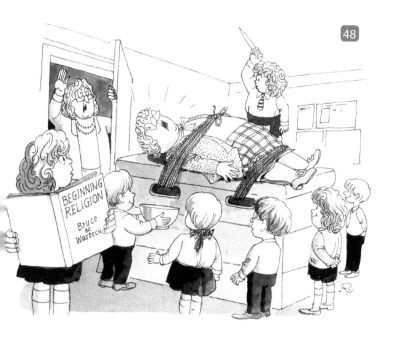

"Release Miss Jones at once, Tracy! I'm sure Mr Bruce and Ms Warbeck meant nothing of the kind!!"

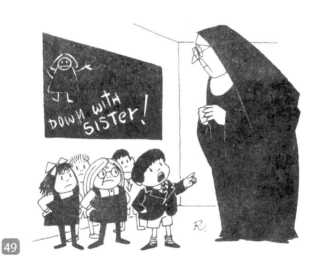

"And if you won't let us do the Little Red School Book for religious instruction . . . we'll resign!"

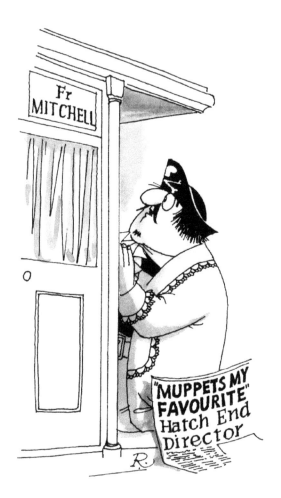

"I committed the sin of envy, Father!"

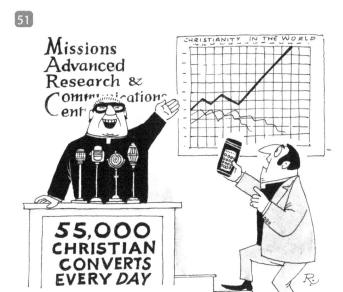

"Hold it! I forgot the decimal point! It should have come before the first 'five'"

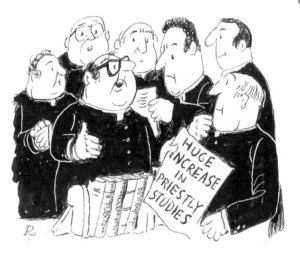

"All celibate . . . no more marriages – no more congregations! . . . end of church!"

53

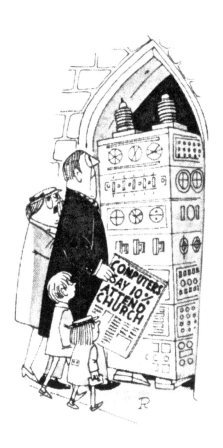

"That must be one of them, dear . . . "

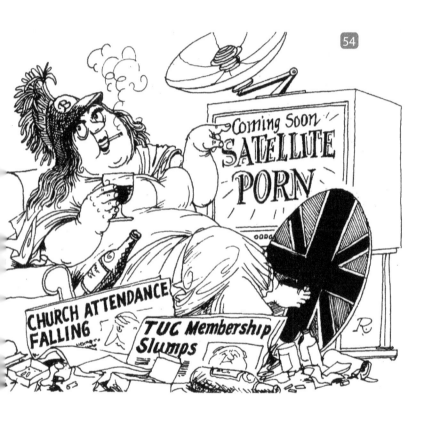

"I mean . . . who wants God and trade unions and all that, when we've got this to look forward to"

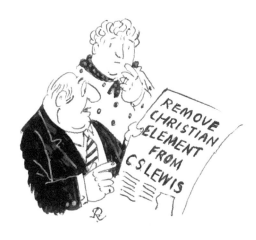

55

" . . . and take God out of the Bible while they're at it!"

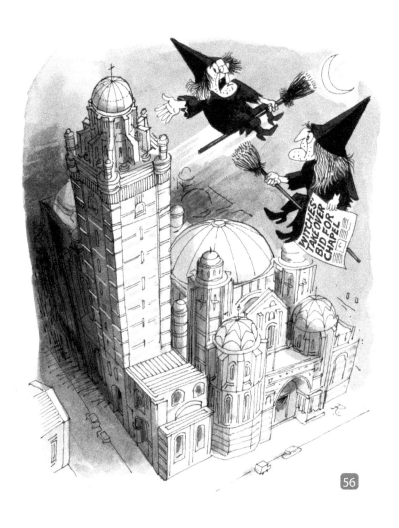

"But I wouldn't touch that one with a broomstick!"

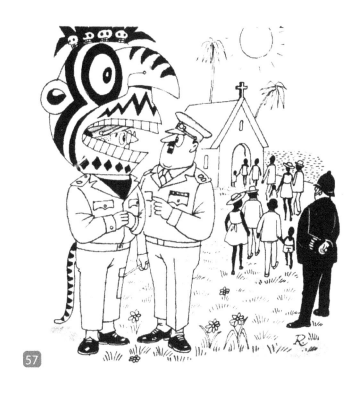

*"Intelligence has boobed again, padre . . . these allegedly
primitive islanders appear to be C. of E., actually"*

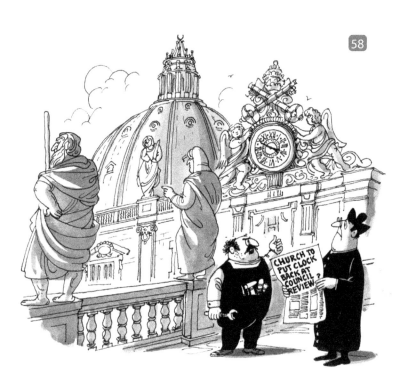

"Hands off this one! It's as much as I can do to keep it going at all!"

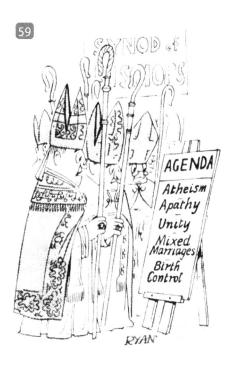

"*Of course, someone's bound to contend that a lot of these problems are too old to be resuscitated!*"

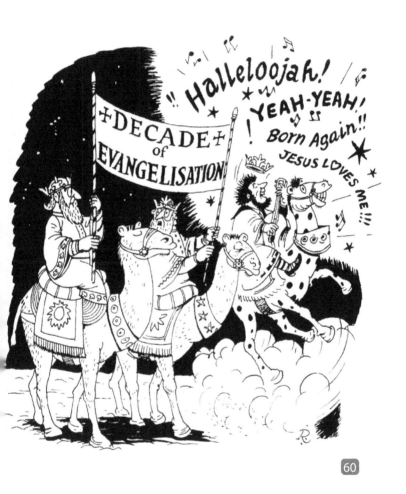

*"Regrettably, one cannot always
choose one's fellow travellers"*

CHAPTER 6

New Waves

Progressive politics and Ecumenism

One of the most important—and now under-
estimated—documents of the Second Vatican Council
was the 1964 Decree *Unitatis Redintegratio*. From an
understanding of Catholicism as the "one true church"
outside of which "there is no salvation", the Council
Fathers acknowledged other "ecclesial communities"
as valid and giving witness to Christ. It also recognized
that despite the Reformation, Catholic traditions might
partially persist in other Christian churches and for this
reason the Anglican Communion "occupies a special
place". The gift of an episcopal ring from Pope Paul VI
to Michael Ramsey, the Archbishop of Canterbury, in
1966 was taken as a palpable sign of these improved
relations. Thereafter, communications between the Pope
and the Archbishop of Canterbury have been open
and often warm. 61 The language of "Mary's Dowry"
and a "Return to Rome" 62 through prayers for the
"Conversion of England" seemed to no longer have a
place within modern ecclesiology.

The foundation of the Anglican-Roman Catholic International Commission (ARCIC) in 1969—whose dry deliberations, John Ryan joked, 63 were not nearly as accessible or popular as the Edinburgh Festival—provided a mechanism for expanding this rapprochement. ARCIC considered many of the thorny areas of theological division, such as papal infallibility and recognition of Anglican ministry. Other areas of advancement included liaising about updated liturgical translations. 64 Yet for all the advances, new faultlines arose; for example, the growing campaign within the Church of England for the ordination of women. 65

At a more grassroots level, British Catholics who had been estranged from the British Council of Churches (BCC) founded by William Temple, Archbishop of Canterbury, in 1942 now looked for opportunities to exchange theological and pastoral perspectives. 66 The high-level thaw in ecumenical relations with all churches 67 was taken further with the Church of England, through the creation in 1967 of a joint BCC/RC working group to study a number of theological issues, including inter-church marriages. Roman Catholics also began to join local Councils of Churches. 68

Yet in some quarters—especially given the long history of anti-Catholicism in Britain, Catholics' perceived deference to a foreign power, and the virulent sectarianism reanimated by the Irish Troubles—clergy like the Reverend Ian Paisley 69 remained strident in their opposition to co-operation and closer union. 70

Older forms of missiology have also since been revived—the rededication of England as the Dowry of Mary in 2020 is perhaps symptomatic of the distance travelled from the ecumenical enthusiasm following the Second Vatican Council through to the sharper denominational lines redrawn in the present day.

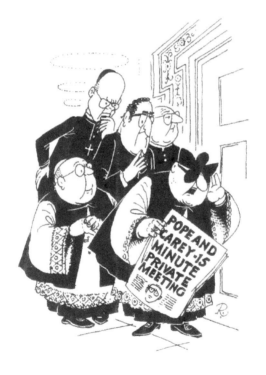

*"How extraordinary! A private meeting . . .
and yet they have to talk in whispers"*

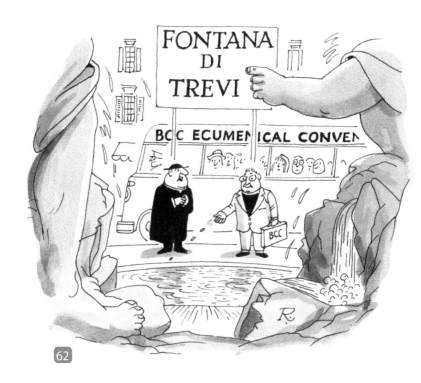

"*The return to Rome which the coins ensure
is of course purely* geographical"

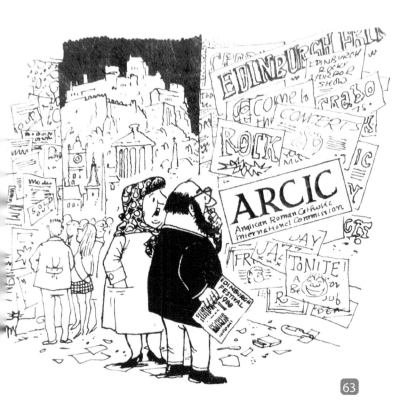

63

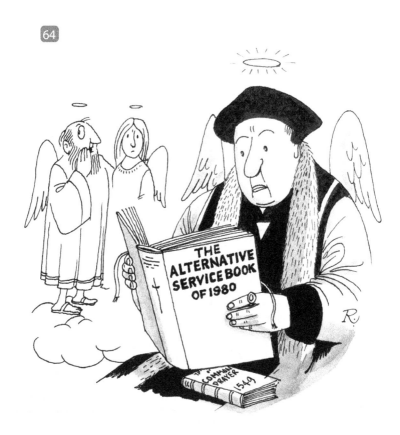

"*Poor old Cranmer . . . another cut
in his spiritual royalties . . .* "

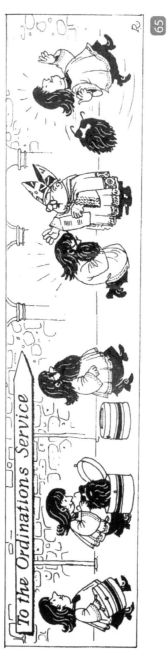

"*I agree . . . bugging would have been less embarrassing for both of us . . .*"

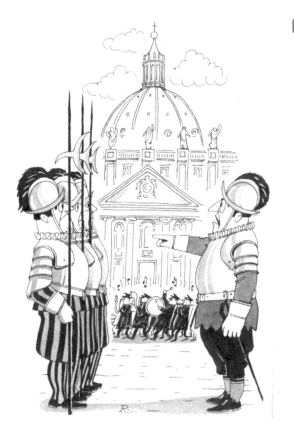

"Volunteers for transfer to the Salvation Army . . . you, you & you!"

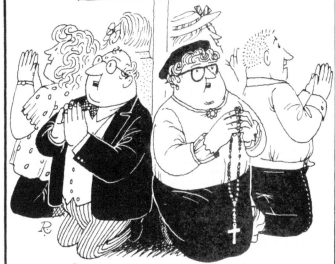

68 **JOHN RYAN**

Unity inauguration report, page 3

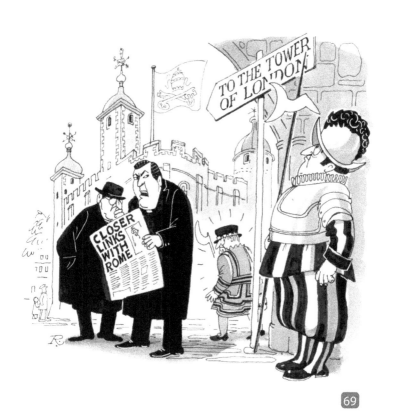

"And what did I tell yez?"

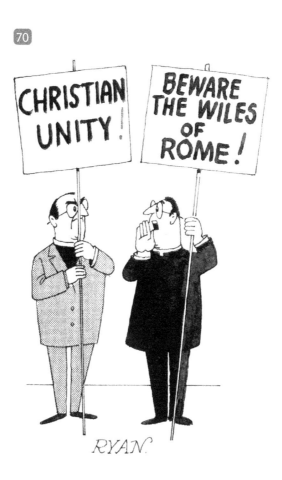

"I've a nasty feeling we've got our banners mixed!"

Captain of the Ship

John Ryan (1921–2009)

The son of a diplomat, John Ryan was born in Edinburgh but educated in the north of England. His lifelong fascination with pirates and the sea—eventually begetting his character *Captain Pugwash*—began in infancy when his family moved to the dynamic port of Rabat in Morocco. At the Catholic boarding school Ampleforth College, where he co-founded a scurrilous "alternative" school magazine, Ryan's witty drawings were encouraged by the art master, an ex-Fleet Street cartoonist. The Second World War intervened, and John fought in Burma. Away from the front line, his wicked caricatures of his superior army officers often got him into hot water.

In 1950, he married fellow artist Priscilla Blomfield, whom he had met at art school in London. Turning down a secure job as art master at Harrow School, (to the horror of his in-laws) he struck out as a freelance commercial artist. As John later explained, he created *Pugwash* and other characters out of financial necessity;

his strip cartoons appeared in *Eagle, Girl,* and *Swift* magazines and the *Radio Times.* His painted murals, TV set designs and light-hearted illustrations were also in demand.

From the late 1950s to the 1970s, John transferred the *Captain Pugwash* stories from page to screen for BBC TV. As Disney-style "stop-frame" animation was beyond his means, he perfected an ingenious method using flat, painted, cardboard characters manipulated with hidden levers. Initially transmitted "live" from the BBC studio, Priscilla was chief lever-puller, while actor Peter Hawkins provided voices for all the characters and sound effects were improvised on the spot. In the very early days, John earned—after expenses—a mere £3 per episode, but the nation took the greedy and cowardly pirate into their hearts and more lucrative animations followed: *The Adventures of Sir Prancelot*; *Mary, Mungo and Midge*; *The Hunting of the Snark* and *The Rime of the Ancient Mariner.*

John was close to his elder brother, the inspirational Fr Columba Ryan OP who was an outstanding teacher and philosopher and for many years at the centre of Dominican intellectual and theological debate. In get-togethers combining hilarity with red wine, John gained acute ecclesiastical insight from his brother. In 1964, Columba introduced John to the *Catholic Herald*'s managing director, Otto Herschan, who—spotting a balanced man able to view an issue from all angles— invited him to be the newspaper's cartoonist. They

both little realized that a cartoon, encapsulating John's funny or poignant comment on the state of the Christian world and beyond, would become his weekly task for the next forty-three years. Initially titled *Drawing it Fine*, weekly instalments often featured "our man in the Vatican", Cardinal Grotti. Readers grew to love this corpulent priest with his puns, sunglasses and eye for the main chance. For John, with a growing houseful of children, relations, lodgers and pets, his fee for the *Catholic Herald* cartoon "kept him in gin". But in the words of the *Catholic Herald*'s outgoing editor on Ryan's retirement, "John's cartoons were his way of serving the Church he loved".

For decades, Ryan's routine was to work in his attic studio from 9am until 6pm, cigarette in one hand (until he dramatically gave up smoking), pen or brush in the other. He had an hour off for lunch, a nap, and a brisk dog-walk. Weekends were for socializing, going to Mass, responding to fans and devising new projects; with holidays spent sketching *en famille*, and walking up mountains in Wales and Italy. Not a born sailor, his Channel crossings in his cousins' small boat were a rich source of exciting nautical misadventures, including being shipwrecked off the Brittany coast.

John and Priscilla moved from London to Rye in the 1980s, but neither "retired". Recreating his attic studio, he wrote and drew more storybooks, happily donating his time and drawings to local charities to raise funds. His colourful and popular *Ark* book series for children

came next, alongside a succession of humorously retold Bible stories, typically championing resourceful youngsters surrounded by foolish adults.

In an interview late in his life Ryan reflected "I'm a lucky man: I've managed to earn a living by doing what I love: drawing and painting every day, supported by my wonderful wife and family."

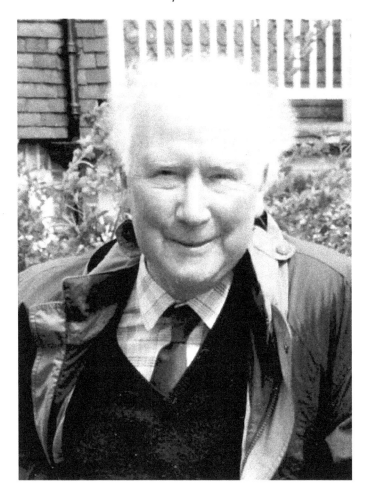

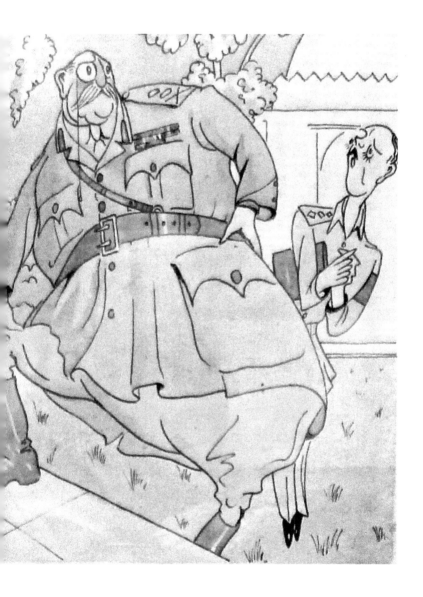

Published in The Services Newspaper of
South East Asia Command, *1943*

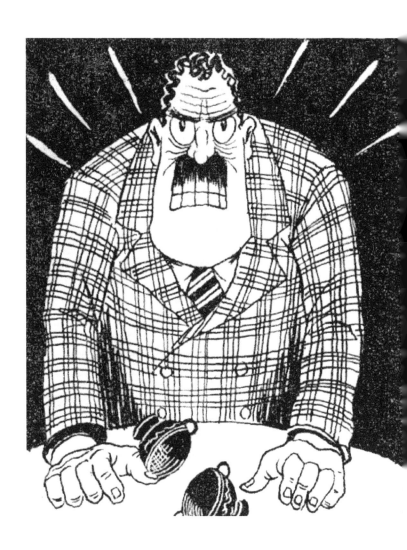

"Harris Tweed" from Eagle *magazine*

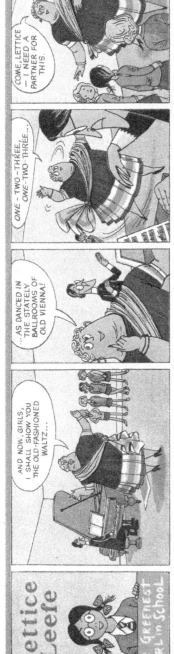
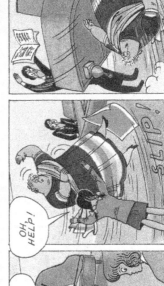
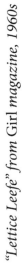

"Lettice Leefe" from Girl magazine, 1960s

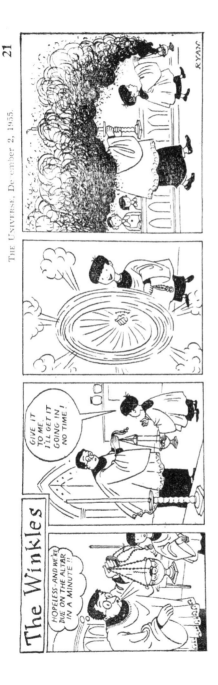

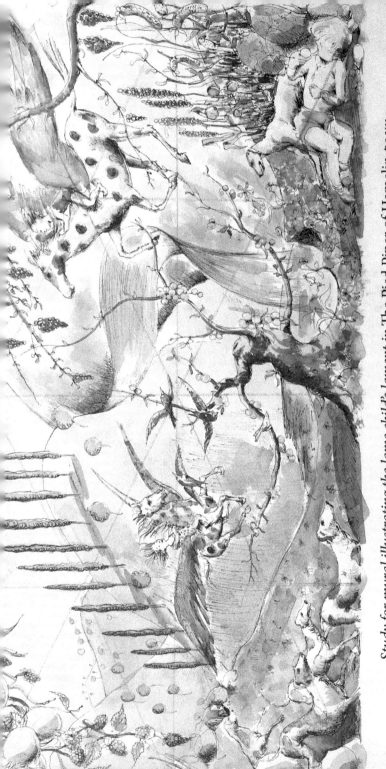

Study for mural illustrating the lame child's lament in The Pied Piper of Hamelin *poem*

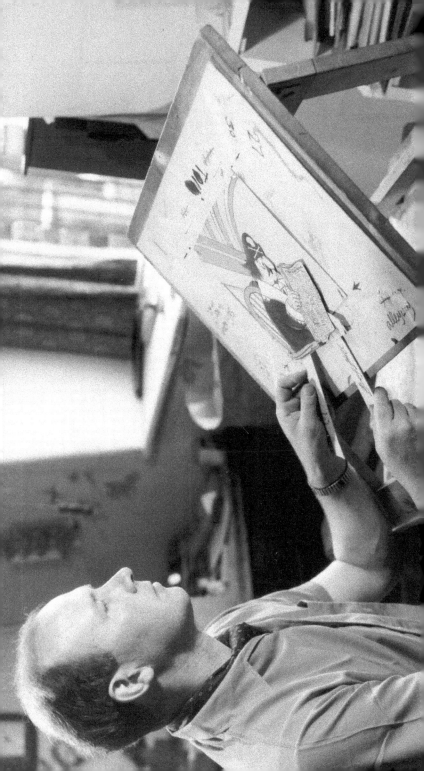

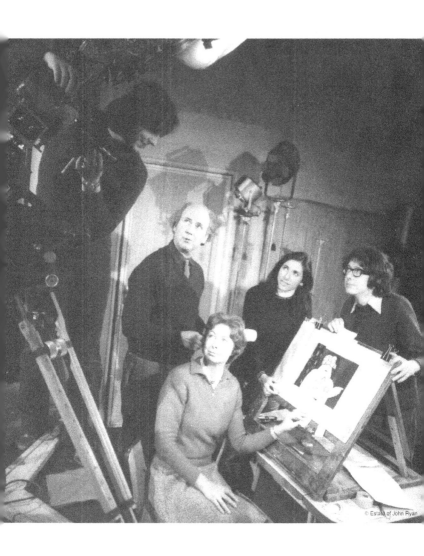

Filming Sir Prancelot *with animation set up ready for camera, 1972*

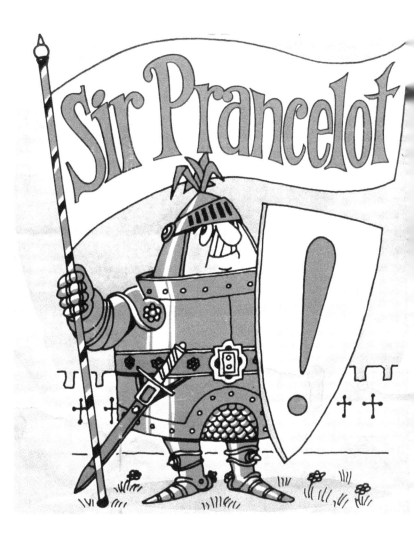

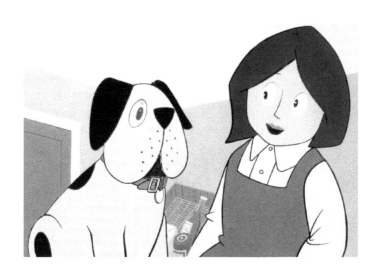

Above: Animations from Mary,
Mungo and Midge, *1960s*

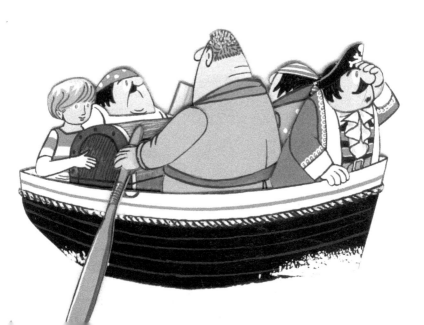

Animations from The Hunting of the Snark *poem, 1960s*

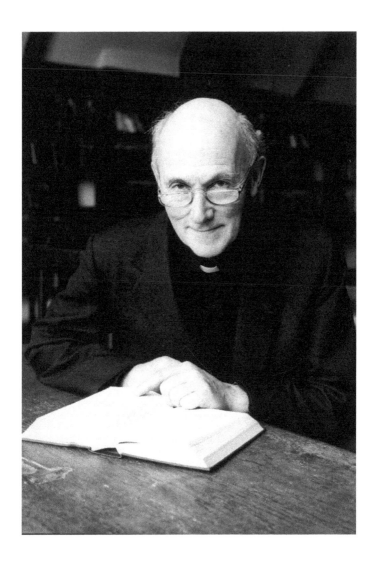

Fr Columba Ryan OP

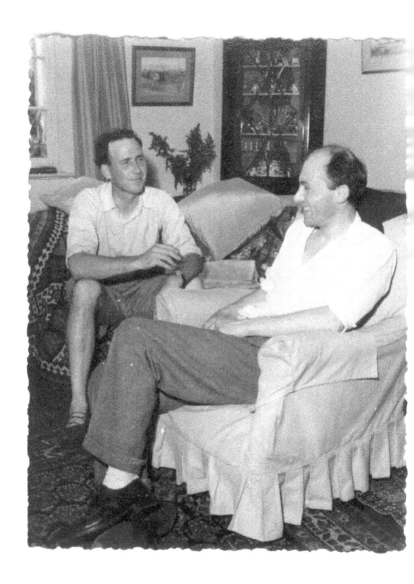

John and Columba, 1950s

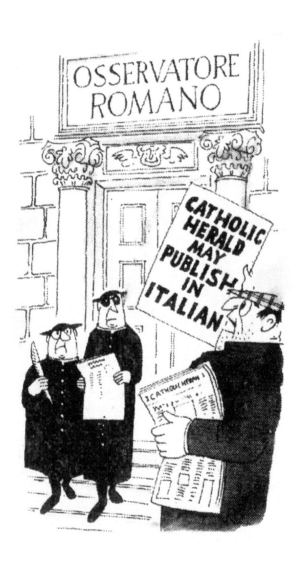

" 'eraldo Cattolico . . . Read all abaht it!"

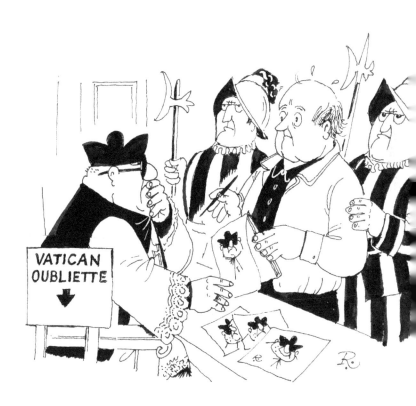

"John Ryan is in Italy . . . He might not return . . . "

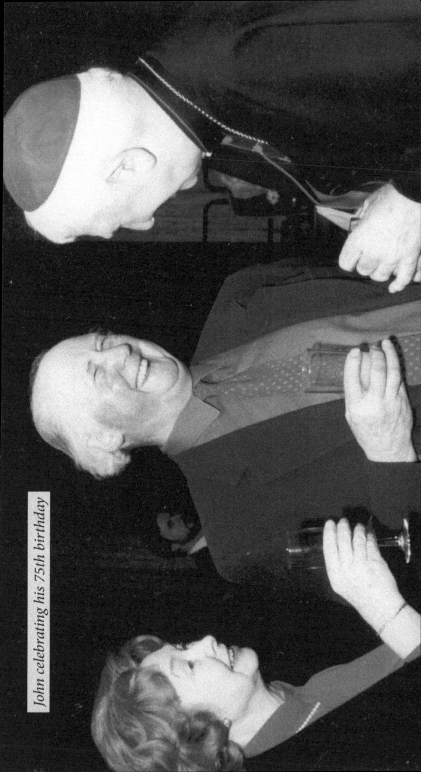

John celebrating his 75th birthday

Cardinal Grott

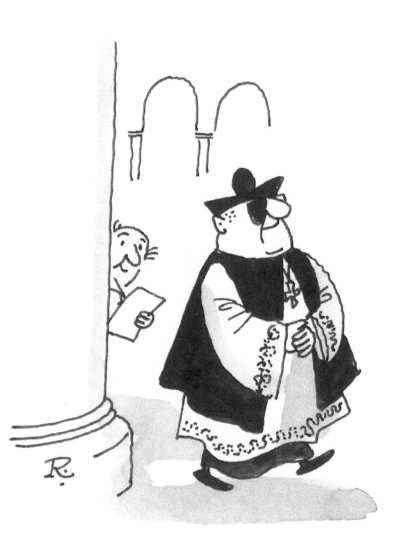

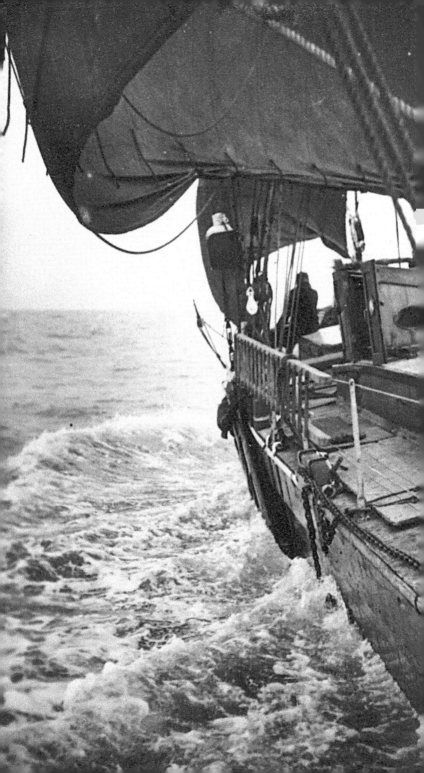

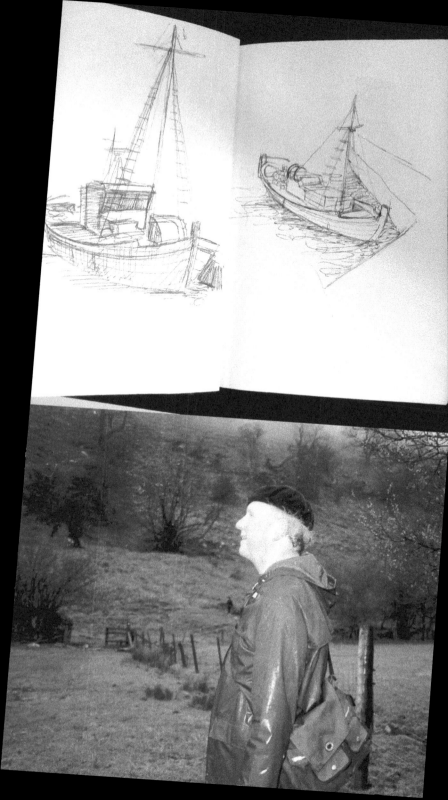

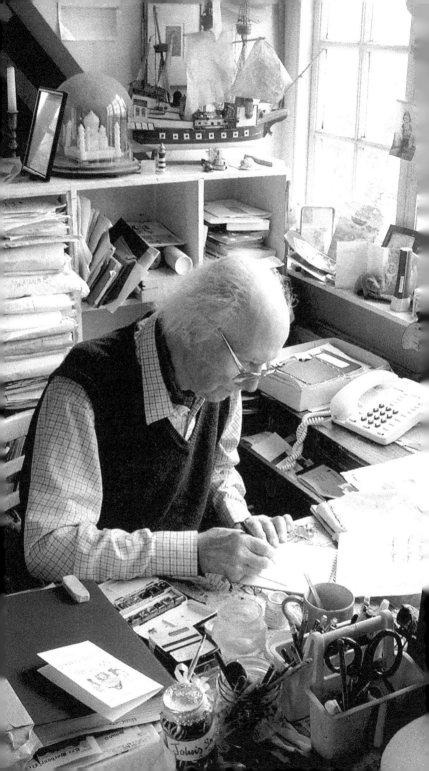

CHAPTER 8

Caught in the Rip?

"There has seldom been a Council
without great confusion after it."
Saint John Henry Newman, 1870

The years surrounding the Second Vatican Council and the corresponding cultural revolution known as "the Sixties" was a tumultuous time for Catholics in Britain, as elsewhere. Hallowed verities, habitual practises and long-established markers of identity were abandoned, refashioned or replaced. This was a period of change and challenge, but also of optimism and experimentation. The Church, and Catholics' place in British society, was transformed and the ordinary person in the pew was confronted by choices.

It was these experiences, emotions and intellectual dilemmas that John Ryan's cartoons brilliantly captured. Laity and clergy alike could accommodate and adapt to the new order, quietly cleave to older ways, or more proactively champion or challenge the post-conciliar agendas. Most people's responses ranged across this spectrum, depending on the aspect of church life

considered. It was rare here, compared to the Continent, to speak consistently of a coherent "traditionalist" or "progressive" camp.

Irrespective of their stance, all agreed that Vatican II was a watershed and that in the years following, the church entered a new era. The tide had shifted irrevocably . . . and one must sink, or swim.

Ryan on Ryan

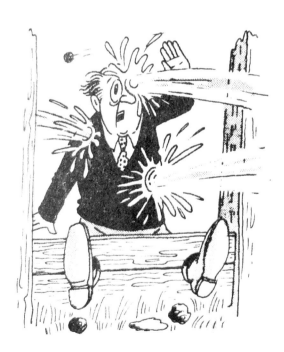

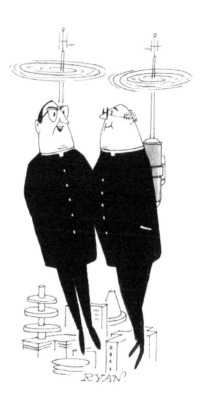

"Extraordinary to think, isn't it, that even as late as the mid-twentieth century Holy Mother Church <u>insisted</u> on a belief in the existence of God . . . "

Author Biographies

Isabel Ryan

Isabel is the younger daughter of the artist and cartoonist John Ryan. She left school at 16, lived briefly on her wits in Paris, ran the information desk at the V&A Museum at weekends and dabbled with design at Chelsea School of Art. At 20, she did a stint as a dogsbody in a Soho design company, then worked in New York City running the office of a French architect rebuilding the Statue of Liberty's flame. Advised by her father never to attempt to earn a living in the Arts world, she has been self-employed for thirty years doing exhibition display graphics for museums and galleries. She manages the John Ryan Estate archive, loaning out Captain Pugwash artworks to pirate-themed exhibitions. She curates displays of her father's work and delights in demonstrating his vintage cardboard TV film animations to a live audience. Brought up a Catholic, with a staunch Anglican mother, she lapsed between the ages of 13 to 47 when, inspired by her family, she returned to the Church.

Alana Harris

Dr Alana Harris is a product of the Australian post-conciliar Church but was immersed from an early age in the devotional life of ultramontane Irish Catholicism by her grandmother and mother. After her first degrees in Law and Italian Renaissance History at the University of Melbourne, she meandered through diverse careers as a reference librarian, corporate lawyer and civil servant. Formative conversations with a holy and quietly progressive Jesuit, followed by a Master of Divinity in an ecumenical seminary for Uniting Church Ministers, female Anglican clergy and Jesuit priests, brought her back to a reconfigured Catholicism. She undertook her doctorate on the reception of the Second Vatican Council and its impact on the devotional lives of English Catholics at Wadham College, Oxford and now teaches Modern British History at King's College London. Her most recent books *Faith in the Family: A Lived Religious History of English Catholicism, 1945–1982* (2013) and *The Schism of '68—Catholicism, Contraception and Humanae Vitae in Europe, 1945–75* (2018) traverse territory covered in this collection.

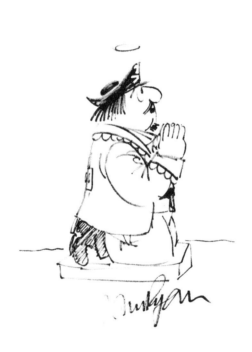